Side mount
PROFILES

The technical diver's guide to side mount diving

Brian Kakuk
& Jill Heinerth

Published by:
Heinerth Productions Inc.
5989 NE County Road 340
High Springs, Fl 32643 USA

First published 2010
Copyright © Jill Heinerth & Brian Kakuk
Photography, illustrations and text
by Jill Heinerth & Brian Kakuk

This manual is not intended to be used as a substitute for proper dive training. Diving is a dangerous sport and training should only be conducted under the safe supervision of an appropriate, active diving instructor until you are fully qualified, and then, only in conditions and circumstances which are as good or better than the conditions in which you were trained. Side mount and cave diving should be taught by a specialized instructor with training credentials and experience in these forms of diving. Careful risk assessment, continuing education and skill practice may lessen your likelihood of an accident, but are never a guarantee for complete safety.

This book assumes a basic knowledge of diving technique and should be used to complement a training course specializing in side mount diving techniques.

Cover Photo: Instructors John Vanderlesst and Linda Claridge at Tank Cave, Australia.

Book design by Heinerth Productions Inc.
www.IntoThePlanet.com

Printed in the USA
ISBN 97809798954

This book is dedicated to the memory of Wes Skiles
in appreciation for his many contributions
to safe cave diving and his boundless passion
for the exploration and protection of springs.

Acknowledgements

Many thanks are expressed to the individuals who agreed to be profiled for this book including Steve Bogaerts, Lamar Hires, Jakub Rehacek and Wes Skiles. We are also greatly indebted to Kristine Rae Olmsted for critical review and proofreading. Her tireless work made this a better book. Our partners in life and business have also supported our efforts to bring this project to completion. Thanks to Robert McClellan, Michelle Brooks, Michael and Nancy Albury for their understanding and support. Steve Bogaerts, Georgia Shemitz, Dive Rite, Wes Skiles and Martyn Farr (Farrworld) offered additional photography to support our efforts. Many divers generously helped us by being models and diving partners including: Scott Bauer, Curt Bowen, Kenny Broad, Kathleen Byers, Linda Clardige, Rich Courtney, Kristi Draper, John Fordor, Richard Dreher, Peter Ekulnd, Mark Goodman, Jeff Gourley, Dimitri Gorsky, Kevin Gurr, Paul Heinerth, Lamar Hires, Hugh Hansard, Matt Hubner, Jitka Hyniova, Tom Iliffe, Kelly Jessup, Jim Killion, Marc Laukien, Dan Lins, Mark Long, Geoffrey May, Tom Morris, Jerry Murphy, Steve Omeroid, Rick Palm, Bill Rennaker, Evgeniy Runkov, David Sawatzky, Nathan Skiles, Wes Skiles, Joel Tower, Terrence Tysall, John Vanderleest, Matt Vinzant, Craig Walters, Mark Wenner, Brian Williams, and Forrest Wilson.

The Authors

BRIAN KAKUK moved to the Bahamas in 1988 after spending 7 years as a U.S. Navy Diver. His work has taken him from the underside of nuclear submarines and aircraft carriers, to jumping from helicopters into gargantuan seas, to record penetrations of underwater cave systems around the world. His research diving work with various governmental and scientific institutions has revealed new species of cave adapted marine life, as well as the discovery of fossils that are now repainting the picture of the Bahamas' past environment. His expertise in diving safety has been called upon by the feature film industry as a Diving Safety Officer and underwater stuntman.

Brian started cave diving in 1990 on Andros Island and is credited with some of the deepest and longest cave dives in the Bahamas.

After working as a civilian contract diver for the U.S. Navy's Atlantic Undersea Test and Evaluation Center (AUTEC), Brian left military research and development diving and moved to the Exuma Cays to take the position of Diving Safety Officer for the Caribbean Marine Research Center on Lee Stocking Island. The caves and deep wall dives in the Exuma Cays proved to be challenging and a perfect environment to learn the scientific significance of the underwater world in the Bahamas.

Brian currently has more than 3000 exploration cave dives to his credit. The use of mixed gas rebreathers, scooters and HID lighting systems have greatly increased the ease of exploration in recent years, but Brian's favorite mode for cave exploration still uses a standard side mounted open circuit configuration.

Brian has authored several articles on exploration, research cave diving, blue hole diving and side mount diving configurations. He is the author of IANTD's Side Mount and No Mount Diver curriculum, currently used by cave diving instructors all over the world, and serves as member of IANTD's International Board of Advisors.

Brian is considered one of the leading authorities on the underwater/underground environments of the Bahamas and is a veteran of multiple high profile underwater cave expeditions in the Bahamas, Mexico and the U.S.

Brian is the founder and Director of the Bahamas Caves Research Foundation. The BCRF provides accurate, cutting edge research on Bahamian blue holes, underwater caves and terrestrial caves, and distributes that information to local and international scientific, governmental and educational institutions. The BCRF will become the liaison between the international scientific community and regulating bodies of the Bahamian Government in order to broker viable, research-based decisions for the conservation and preservation of Bahamian underground environments.

Bahamas Underground
www.bahamasunderground.com
Bahamas Caves Research Foundation
www.bahamascaves.com

JILL HEINERTH is an explorer. For over twenty years, her curiosity and photographic skills have given us a tantalizing peek at a breathtaking underwater world few will ever experience.

Best known as a pioneering technical diver, Jill combines a mastery of underwater technology with a formal Fine Arts education to produce artistic documentation of the natural environment above, below and inside our planet.

An award-winning filmmaker, Jill co-wrote, produced, and appeared in *Water's Journey,* the PBS documentary series that takes viewers on visceral travels through the world's greatest water systems. Hollywood directors call on her to produce difficult underwater scenes and international magazines and websites look to her to document extreme environments with high technology.

Jill is a reasonable voice in the world of conservation, and is often sought out for insightful commentary by the media, government, and academic institutions.

Jill's many diving accomplishments are highlighted by an Antarctic cave diving expedition inside B-15, the largest iceberg known to humankind (National Geographic - *Ice Island*), and significant contributions to the United States Deep Caving Team's *Wakulla 2* project, which used paradigm-changing technology to map an underwater cave system in three dimensions. At Wakulla, secondary to a scientific mission, Jill established a women's diving world record.

Some of Jill's numerous professional diving, photographic and filmmaking awards include: *Sport Diving* Magazine - Named A Living Legend, Women Diver's Hall of Fame - Inaugural Inductee, Explorer's Club Film Festival - Best Documentary, Canadian Technical Diver of the Year and Fellow - National Speleological

Society as well as top honors from the International HD Film Fest, Cine Golden Eagle, and Aurora Awards. Jill was also honored by Keen Footwear as a top environmental photographer, bringing attention to the crisis of diminishing freshwater resources.

Jill Heinerth holds various SCUBA, cave diving, and closed circuit rebreather instructor credentials. An *Adobe Photoshop* expert, she also teaches specialized underwater digital photography workshops and classes. With a wealth of experience as a former owner of a Toronto ad agency, Jill accepts select advertising clients, applying her distinct skill set to each application.

Jill gives upbeat, entertaining, and informative multimedia presentations to groups, clubs and organizations on a wide range of subjects including exploration, motivation and actualization, conservation, risk management and filmmaking.

Born in Canada, Jill lives with her husband, Robert, in Florida, where she starts most days with a refreshing swim in the clear water of her local spring.

www.IntoThePlanet.com
www.RebreatherPro.com

Table of Contents

INTRODUCTION

CHAPTER

Chapter One

Not Just for Explorers

In recent years, side mount diving has progressed more than any other aspect of our sport. Divers have come to recognize that this versatile configuration is one of the most comfortable, stable and safe ways to enjoy the underwater world.

Though the system originated and was once the exclusive territory of a certain "lunatic fringe" of cave divers (otherwise known as our friends and mentors), side mount is becoming increasingly popular with very safe (and sane) open water and wreck divers. Even Closed Circuit Rebreather divers choose streamlined side mounted tanks for both open water and cave bailout configurations.

Before we "dive" into the text, a little history is in order. Over the last 40-plus years, underwater cave exploration has expanded by leaps and bounds. Improved technology has fueled much of this journey. Smaller, lighter, and longer-lasting underwater lighting has contributed greatly to reducing a diver's profile. Advanced dive computers, capable of multi-gas and multi-algorithm profiling, has made technical and decompression diving safer and more efficient. Equipment continues to change and become more streamlined, as well as more mission-specific. Diver Propulsion Vehicles (DPVs), have pushed the

line, allowing the penetration of record caves to be measured in miles, rather than feet. With the benefits of this newly acquired technology, divers continue to hone techniques and practices allowing them to safely reach deeper, longer, and smaller spaces inside the earth's underwater and underground environments. Side mount diving has contributed greatly to this remarkable paradigm shift in underwater exploration.

Australian cave diving instructors John Vanderleest and Linda Claridge slip through passages in Tank Cave in Australia's Mount Gambier region. Low-ceiling caves such as this are ideal for side mount configuration.

The intent of this text is to provide information on the latest versions of equipment, techniques, and recognized safety protocols, enabling divers to pursue open water, wreck and cave diving (at any level), using the side mount configuration. It is not the intent of the authors that this text provide stand-alone training in the use of side mount diving equipment or techniques. The reader is cautioned that the information provided is designed to be integrated with a structured side mount diving course, given by a certified and qualified Side Mount Open Water or Side Mount Cave Diving Instructor who is sanctioned by an industry-recognized training agency.

At the time of this writing, the following agencies provide formal training in Side Mount Cave Diving:

International Association of Nitrox and Technical Divers (IANTD), National Association for Cave Diving (NACD), National Speleological Society/Cave Diving Section (NSS/CDS). The following agencies provide training and certification in Side Mount Open Water Diving: International Association of Nitrox and Technical Divers (IANTD), and the Professional Association of Diving Instructors (PADI).

Opposite: During exploration, a side mount harness may take quite a bit of abuse, as is the case with this rig, after sump exploration in Roppel Cave, Kentucky.

Safe Diving,
Brian and Jill

HISTORY

CHAPTER

2

The Evolution of Side Mount Diving Technique

The first departure from standard back mounted cylinders occurred beneath the hills of northern England in the early 1960s. British cave diver Mike Boon, having recently ditched double hose regulators for the newly designed single hose regulator, made an attack on the sumps of Hardrawkin Pot in Yorkshire, England, using an unconventional tactic. Slinging the cylinder on his side, with a bandoleer-style harness, he was able to easily slip through restrictions which were considered impassable with back mounted kit. This new-found configuration would allow exploration in many other British systems that had previously been considered too small for exploration with current technology.

The mode of passing sumps during that time period was simply a matter of strapping on some sort of breathing apparatus (often a war surplus oxygen rebreather), and hiking and pulling oneself along the bottom and walls of the submerged passage. It wasn't until the early to mid 1960s that British cave divers even decided to use fins rather than boots while passing sumps. The often-dark water of the sumps created an environment where consideration of anti-silting techniques seemed pointless, so buoyancy control devices were not a priority.

Wes Skiles diving in an earlier version of Dive Rite's TransPac system.

As necessity is the mother of invention, one impetus for side mount diving in North America came from a much darker episode. In the late 1970s, an untrained diver had managed to fatally slide into an impossibly narrow crevice in Royal Spring in North Florida. Divers Sheck Exley and Wes Skiles, two of the most experienced cave divers in the area were tasked with the recovery of the wedged diver.

After several unsuccessful attempts at recovering the diver using back mounted cylinders, Exley concocted a single cylinder rig with a hose clamp and belt. Holding the cylinder at his side, he slid into the crevice beside the dead diver, breaking him loose from the cave's grasp.

Skiles, seeing this configuration in action, quickly realized the possibilities of a similar setup for exploration of smaller passages, and thus, side mount cave exploration began to expand through the US.

In 1977, cave diver Forrest Wilson adopted a belt-style rig to carry two independent cylinders. Active in sump diving, he learned about the technique from British sump explorers who used it to efficiently transit tanks through the cave and then dive. Soon after, Wilson added bicycle inner tubes to hold the tops of his tanks, a technique he was shown by Woody Jasper.

In the late 1970s, Skiles and Jasper began toying with harness and buoyancy devices that would allow them to carry independent and thus redundant cylinders on their sides, and at the same time, stay off of the floor of the cave. Inspired by Rory Dickens and his book *The Physics and Engineering of Diving,* their goal was to bring the tanks forward and align them along the diver's longitudinal and lateral axis. The movement of the tanks forward, and the incorporation of the buoyancy devices, was where the British and North American gear parted in concept.

Proper buoyancy and trim is now the foundation of cave diving technique, and the ability to stay off of the floor of the cave allowed the divers to maintain the good visibility Florida caves are known for.

Skiles took a US Divers horse-collar BCD and attached it to the front of an Atpack wing. This increased lift while adjusting the diver's trim to a more horizontal position, as well as allowing a space for the side mounted cylinders to lay. He later used a Scubapro stab jacket to achieve similar results. During an exploration dive into Gator Cave, in Merritt's Mill Pond, he was able to pass several restrictions which had previously stopped he and other back mount divers. After laying 360 feet of line in ex-

Forrest Wilson and friends diving at Black Lagoon in Hart Springs Park, Gilchrist County, Florida.

In other parts of the world, divers such as David Sawatzky modified the system designed by Woody Jasper, using it to explore significant, remote side mount passages in Ontario and British Columbia, Canada.

Lamar Hires in Japan with his earliest TransPac.

tremely small passage, Skiles realized that this configuration was a real exploration tool. He termed the rig "double-singles," and the first real side mount exploration in North America had begun in earnest.

In the following years, a close knit group of divers, including Skiles, Court Smith, Mark Long, Tom Morris, Woody Jasper and Lamar Hires continued pushing small caves and making modifications to their equipment. The group became known throughout the cave diving community as the "Mole Tribe," for their escapades into smaller and smaller caves. In the mid 80s, Woody Jasper and Ron Simmons made significant progress with the trim and balance of the side mount setup by figuring out how to keep the cylinders horizontal while also maintaining the shoulder of the cylinder higher and closer to the diver's body. Ron's hinged "I" plate integrated with entrapped wings and harness systems, was the first truly workable rig that could be replicated.

In 1995, Dive Rite released the TransPac as a solution for remote sump diving exploration that

Lamar Hires was conducting in Japan. Soon after, they began selling modified versions of the modular diving harness set up for side mounting. This became the first "off-the-rack" side mount system available to the diving community.

Since that time, Dive Rite's TransPac system has morphed into the Nomad and Nomad EXP, and other

systems, such as Brett Hemphill's Armadillo side mount harness (now produced by Golem Gear), have evolved. These two rigs are the most prominent off-the-rack systems.

Side mount pioneer Woody Jasper diving in Bluebird Cave in 1984. Photo: Wes Skiles

Divers all over the world embrace side mount. Here, John Vanderleest dives at The Pines in Australia.

GETTING STARTED

CHAPTER **3**

Training Prerequisites

Side mount diving can be broken down into several levels of training; thus prerequisites vary by level.

Open Water Side Mount

Side mount configuration is used for various activities in open water technical diving such as wreck diving, deep and wall diving. It is recommended that divers seeking training in the use of this configuration be trained in the use of Nitrox and staged decompression, since the use of double cylinders may expose the diver to profiles requiring the use of these disciplines.

Cave Diver in Side Mount Configuration

Side mount configuration as a style of double cylinders is gaining in popularity for people with no intention of accessing small restrictions or "side mount" sized passages. This style of diving may be incorporated into entry-level cavern and cave diving courses if permitted by your specific training agency standards. No advanced side mount diving techniques (i.e. cylinder removals, accessing side mount restrictions or side mount passages) will be presented at this level of training. Prerequisites for entry-level cavern and cave training vary by training agency, but generally require Advanced Open Water and usually Nitrox foundations in diving.

Side Mount Cave Diver

This course exposes trained cave divers to the use of side mount configuration in smaller side mount caves as well as skills including cylinder removal, portage of cylinders, gas planning for slow exit scenarios such as restrictions, low visibility and system malfunctions. Prerequisites for this course are Full Cave Diver certification, a minimum of 50 non-training cave dives after Full Cave Diver certification and that the diver be at least 18 years of age.

Previously the domain of cave explorers, side mount technique is finding its way into all facets of diving.

Advanced Side Mount Cave Diver

This course exposes the qualified, experienced cave diver to techniques and configurations that allow them to safely make full use of side mount configuration, including cylinder removals for accessing very small restrictions and passages, the use of single and double stage cylinders, and planning more technical dives. It is highly recommended that divers entering this level of training have completed a minimum of 50 cave dives after completion of their Full Cave Course, Side Mount Course, have a Nitrox certification and be at least 18 years of age.

Many Closed Circuit Rebreather (CCR) divers integrate side mount harnesses and/or bungees into their unit to allow for improved streamlining of bailout tanks.

Suggested Equipment

In addition to tanks, the following list includes the basic equipment needed for any side mount diving rig. (* indicates additional gear for overhead environments such as caves or wrecks.)

Harness

The harnesses listed below are good commercially available choices for side mount diving, though some are more regional and mission specific than others. The Armadillo and Nomad harness systems have been available for several years and have established a strong following. Newer to the

The side mount harness is your support structure. It provides the appropriate connection points for carrying two tanks parallel to your body. In most cases, the harness is equipped with an air cell, which provides lift without sacrificing a trim profile.

market are the Razor, Oxycheq Recon, and the Hollis SMS 100. Their individual specifications may be viewed on the respective manufacturer's website.

Tanks

Steel LP85 cft. (12 L) cylinders are one of the most popular tanks because of their weight and buoyancy characteristics. Aluminum 80s (11 L) and neutral Aluminum 72s are popular with wet suit divers in warm water locations. Larger capacity tanks are not as popular and can be too negatively buoyant for most air cells.

Regulators

Good, high-performance DIN regulators should be used, and each regulator should be considered for the following:
- Breathing performance at deeper depths associated with technical and overhead environment diving.
- Compatibility with Nitrox and other mixed gases that are used on technical dives.
- Hose-routing for side mount configuration. First stage regulators with swivel style bodies that allow multiple low pressure hose configurations are ideal.
- Right-angle adapters on second stages. These allow the hoses to take a natural placement, which reduces jaw fatigue on longer dives and makes the hose more snag-resistant by keeping the second stage hose close to the diver's body. Note: these are hard-angle adapters and not two-piece spherical swivels, which are considered a weak link in the gas system.

High Pressure Gauges and Hoses

Each regulator should have its own submersible pressure gauge. Brass and glass gauges with 6-inch high pressure hoses are preferred by side mount divers. Small, micro gauges work but larger, 2-inch brass and glass gauges are easier to find and read.

Exposure Protection

You will need appropriate exposure protection for the area and environment in which you will be diving. Remember that when a diver increases their gas supply by using two cylinders, bottom times and potential decompression obligation will increase submersion time. Side mount divers should plan appropriate thermal protection for extended bottom times and decompression, regardless of whether they are diving in warm open water, caves or colder climates.

Wetsuits offer a lower overall profile, but drysuits offer the advantage of being able to shift air within the suit to affect trim. Drysuit divers will need to be mindful of air trapping in the legs if they expect to encounter head-down restrictions and chimneys. Leg gaitors may reduce the likelihood of air being trapped in the feet.

Cutting Devices

There are many styles of cutting devices that are appropriate for specific types of diving, however the era of the giant Rambo knife is long gone. Knives worn on the leg are difficult to access while wearing side mount cylinders, and are a significant snag hazard in caves or on wrecks. Options such as harness-stowed or pocket-stowed cutting devices are much more appropriate. Offshore divers should consider placing a small knife in a pocket or on the harness, or using a pair of emergency cutting shears stowed in a sheath, either on the harness or in a pocket.

Cave divers, who are more prone to line entanglement, may opt for a simple Z-knife (parachute cord cutter) stowed on the harness or on a wrist mounted computer band. A backup knife in a pocket or detachable pouch is also recommended. Smaller titanium blade backup knives are an excellent choice since they do not corrode, hold a fine edge and are easily stowed in an accessory pocket or on the harness.

Lights*

Primary Lights - Small canister HID lights or comparable LED lights work well for side mounting. The main objective is to reduce size, while maintaining a dependable beam and substantial

A titanium Z-knife.

Recent developments in lighting have allowed for small primary lights to be carried with or without a separate battery pack.

Low profile helmets should fit snugly over a neoprene hood, or have a proper suspension system. Foam interiors should be avoided.

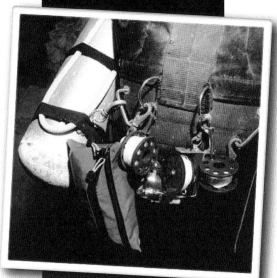

A cave diver's pocket and reels, stowed on the back of the harness.

burn time. The placement of such lights will be covered later in the text.

Backup Lights – Compact backup lights are recommended and LED technology is most popular. Many divers avoid lights that use external switches since they contain a secondary failure point. Bezel type on/off or magnetic switch mechanisms may be more reliable and less prone to flooding. Small LED lights can be harness- or helmet-mounted.

Reels*

The side winder or Jasper-style primary reel offers the lowest profile for a primary or exploration reel. With the exception of primary and exploration reels, finger spools, rather than reels, are preferred. Spools are less prone to jamming or entanglement. Many manufacturers offer finger spools in various sizes including safety spools, jump/gap spools, and mini jump spools. Most side mount divers will carry a minimum of two finger spools.

Line Arrows and Markers*

Cave divers are required to carry a minimum of three line arrows and three non-directional markers. In side mount diving, these are often stowed carefully in a pocket on a bungee and clip.

Optional Equipment

*Helmet** - Although helmets are not popular in North Florida, they are useful and accepted in most other regions. Helmets may be especially important for exploration divers traveling in the smallest passages where loose rock can injure a diver. Many divers mount their backup lights on their helmet and often employ a quick-receiver that can hold their primary light. If you are task loaded by photography or survey work, these lights are extremely useful. More importantly, a helmet protects the diver's head while they work in restricted spaces or utilize Diver Propulsion Vehicles (DPVs).

Pocket - Accessory gear may be carried in an independent pocket. The pocket can be clipped and stowed on a rear D-ring located on the waist, on the back of the harness. The clipped pocket allows for easy access to all of the contents, rather than digging blindly in a side or thigh pocket, hoping to reach the correct piece of equipment.

Dive Computers - There are numerous dive computers on the market that work well for open water, wreck and cave diving, and the model chosen should be researched with your specific type of diving in mind. With side mount diving, a computer that can handle multiple Nitrox mixes or even Trimix gases is strongly recommended. Even if you are not currently using Nitrox or Trimix, your experience may eventually lead you to this type of diving, and it can get expensive to have different computers for different types of diving. Your side mount instructor can help you make a well-informed decision on dive computer purchases. Cave explorers may consider a dive computer that features audible alerts, which aid the diver in low or no-visibility scenarios.

Backup Dive Computers – Whenever staged decompression dives are conducted (this will happen in most wreck or cave diver classes), you need to have some sort of backup decompression information. This can be achieved by purchasing a second computer, or by carrying decompression tables with a digital bottom timer and backup depth gauge.

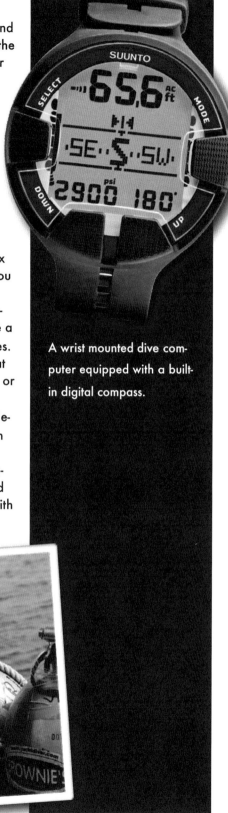

A wrist mounted dive computer equipped with a built-in digital compass.

GEAR STYLES

CHAPTER 4

Martyn Farr's Explorer Harness. The lower end of the tank is attached at either (A) or (B) - moveable around the waist. Bungee runs from (C), which is also used to fix the wing; this clips to (B) while the harness is put on, then moved under the arm to (D). The tank is swung upright and the bungee captures the cylinder valve to hold it in place against the body before being clipped to (D). Dive reels are attached to (E).

Harness System Styles

Belt Systems

Belt systems were some of the first methods to be used and are the easiest to configure. Though several designs exist, the basic structure includes a harness and waist strap system that allows cylinders to be slung on the sides using D-ring attachment points on the waist or rear, via extensions, while the top of the cylinders are held in place with a stretchy bungee of some type.

These harnesses generally do not include buoyancy compensators but they may be added as an after-market modification. Belt harnesses are the most streamlined of all of the current side mount systems when used in their base configuration, with lightweight aluminum cylinders in shallow water.

Current versions adapt well to the dry caving environment and are generally used by sump divers for traversing water-filled sections of dry caves. For cave diving in general, a BCD should be added to accommodate heavier steel cylinders and deeper dives. A buoyancy device is mandatory for open water diving. Once a BCD is retrofitted, there is little difference in profile between this and other home made or off-the-rack designs.

Homemade Jacket Style

Many side mount configurations have been and continue to be highly modified harnesses made from open water diving equipment. The foundation of the first North American systems were larger capacity buoyancy "stab" jackets that were modified by incorporating web harnesses, mounting plates, brackets, D-rings, clips, inner tubes, bungee cords and the like. Most current homemade systems are fashioned from off-the-rack systems, with an outer, soft harness and some sort of "captured" wing system that is placed between the diver and the harness. This facilitates a very low profile, however captured wing systems do have an issue with air trapping when the BCD bladder gets pinched under the harness straps, making it difficult or inconvenient to move air around or out of the bladder.

The possible innovations to this type of system seem limitless. This type of harness system can be just as streamlined as the other systems and with the proper choice of BCD, can accommodate steel and multiple cylinder configurations.

Off-The-Rack

The last 10 years have seen great advancements in "off-the-rack" or commercially-available side mount harness and air cell systems. There are currently two commercially available systems that, based on sales, are the most popular with cave divers: the Dive Rite Nomad/Nomad EXP and Golem Gear's Armadillo Side Mount System.

In the early 1990s, Dive Rite Manufacturing developed the modular TransPac harness system and by the mid 1990s they began selling add-on components to adapt their TransPac into a side mount configuration.

The system has now evolved into their Nomad and Nomad EXP line and is a popular system among both novice and experienced side mount divers. One particular benefit of the Nomad is that it incorporates a 60 lb. wing for divers carrying heavier tanks. The modular fit covers a wide range of body types.

Another pioneering off-the-rack model is the Armadillo Side Mount Harness, now marketed by Golem Gear Inc. The first versions of the Armadillo harness were designed by cave diver Brett Hemphill around 1997 for use in the smaller passages of spring caves in Florida. With the support of Curt Bowen from Advanced Diver Magazine, the first production runs of the Armadillo were sewn together at Zeagle Manufacturing. Production was eventually taken over by Golem Gear, and the units are now assembled in the Czech Republic and imported to the United States.

The Armadillo is the only non-captured wing on the market right now and was the first system to use

One of Bill Rennaker's early side mount rigs which used a sport diving BCD and a special aluminum hip plate to secure the lower end of the tanks.

Bill Rennaker, owner of Cave Excursions dive shop in Florida.

The Dive Rite Nomad EXP is an all-in-one design, while the Nomad XT is modular, capturing the wing under the harness.

the "butt plate" extension that lowers the attachment point on the harness. The Armadillo is a popular system among exploration cave divers. It is the only design that incorporates an optional climbing/rappelling harness into the system. Equipped with a certified canyoneering harness, it can withstand the rigors of moisture and wear. As such, it is preferred by many sump divers.

Newcomers to the side mount market include the Oxycheq Recon and Hollis SMS100. These systems use the captured wing concept with a soft harness and detachable "butt plate" that allows cylinders to be mounted lower on the torso, but higher in terms of the center of gravity of the diver.

Pros & Cons of Various Styles

There are pros and cons with each of the above systems. Divers must judge each system's merits against the the diving environments they encounter, consider how much money they can commit to their system and assess the availability of repair parts. Side mount diving in small caves is exceedingly hard on equipment, and the ability to fix and/or replace part(s) of the system is critical. The overall profile and complexity of a system will also limit the size of cave that a diver can access. Additional features and high lift capacity bladders may significantly increase the travel and profile size of the diver.

Belt/Harness Systems

Belt/harness systems are the least expensive and easiest systems to fabricate. They are the most streamlined of all the systems. This system is commonly used with aluminum cylinders and thus a large buoyancy device may not be needed to offset negative buoyancy. This type of rig works well in shallow caves where there are no dramatic changes in depth throughout the dive.

For larger cylinders, steel tanks or caves with greater depths or depth changes, a buoyancy device must be incorporated into the harness, or the weight of the cylinders will sink the diver to the floor, as well as making a horizontal attitude in the cave nearly impossible. Open water divers must also use a buoyancy device with this system.

The use of aluminum cylinders creates challenges due to inherent change in buoyancy of the cylinder throughout the dive. As the gas is used in each cylinder, the bottom becomes lighter and the cylinder shifts to float in a valve-down position. This places the delicate regulator and valve toward the floor of the cave where it will more readily snag on projections, and puts the bottom of the cylinder pointing up, where it creates more drag and can break fragile ceiling formations.

Some divers who prefer this system, or who use aluminum cylinders, have created a second, lower attachment point on the waist-belt of the harness. When the aluminum cylinders become lighter throughout the dive, the bottom cylinder clip is moved to the lower attachment point, keeping the cylinder in a horizontal attitude despite the buoyancy change.

One drawback to this system is that for any cylinders other than aluminum 80 cft (or smaller), a buoyancy device or drysuit must be incorporated into the system for lift. At this point the system loses its prominence as the most streamlined system.

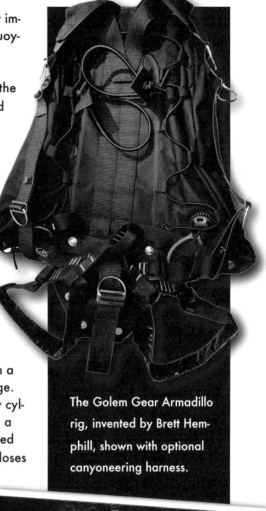

The Golem Gear Armadillo rig, invented by Brett Hemphill, shown with optional canyoneering harness.

Off-the-Rack Harness Systems

Off-the-Rack Harness systems are the most popular choice of cave and open water divers moving into side mount diving. With different options for lift and streamlining, these side mount systems can handle many different cylinder options with regard to size and weight. There are some differences in lifting capacities between various models, so the basic principals in buoyancy capacity vs. profile may play a part in the purchasing decision.

If a diver expects to carry large steel cylinders or multiple cylinders for stage diving, then a high volume lift, larger profile system may be the right choice. If the diver plans to work in extremely con-

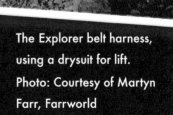

The Explorer belt harness, using a drysuit for lift.
Photo: Courtesy of Martyn Farr, Farrworld

33

Kristi Draper experiments with small steel 45 cft tanks.

When configured properly, a side mount harness is capable of staging additional aluminum tanks.

fined spaces, or with medium sized cylinders, then one of the lower profile, lower volume systems would be in order. There is no way to avoid the basic physics of the fact that if lift is increased, then so is the profile.

One of the few drawbacks to the off-the-rack air cell system is the tendency for part of the air cell to form a "bubble" on the shoulder/back of the diver when lifting heavy or multiple cylinders. The bubble increases the front to back profile and can snag on overhead projections in tight passages or restrictions. This usually occurs in a place (right between the shoulder blades) that is very difficult to reach. Divers should make efforts to rig this system properly in order to minimize this problem, by taking advantage of the bungee constricting systems incorporated into the top of the harness. These bungees can be tightened, which constricts the top of the wing and forces air to the bottom sections of the air bladder. This gives greater lift to the hip region, where it is most needed.

There are a few additional ways to increase or decrease the volume needed for buoyancy in the side mount wing:

- Use of a drysuit – Often the drysuit is used for buoyancy and the BCD of the harness system is considered the redundant backup. The diver shifts air within the drysuit to achieve good trim.
- Use of semi-drysuit – These thicker suits often add just enough buoyancy to assist with the use of larger cylinders.
- Saltwater vs. Freshwater – Diving in saltwater gives additional buoyancy, allowing for larger cylinders or the addition of a stage cylinder without stressing the bladder of the buoyancy system.
- Addition of external or integrated weight systems for both decreased buoyancy and trim. This is often an option for drysuit divers or larger divers.

There are some models which are better suited for certain body types. There are even specific designs that are intended for smaller divers. It is important that the diver consult with a reputable side mount instructor prior to purchasing one of these systems. Dive shop personnel may not have specific experience in fitting side mount rigs. Make inquiries about background and experience before trusting a critical fit decision to someone other than your instructor.

Once a system has been purchased, the next and most important step is proper adjustment and sizing. This step should be made with the assistance of an experienced side mount instructor. Proper adjustment can be tedious in the first dive or two, but once the adjustments are made properly, the rest of the system including cylinder placement, accessory placement and access, as well as buoyancy and trim all fall easily into place. Without assistance with this first step, the diver is in for a long and frustrating learning curve. More than other gear configurations, fitting of side mount gear may come down to micro adjustments that make large changes in trim. These

The Hollis SMS100 is one of the newest all-in-one units to come to the market.

micro adjustments need to be done in the water, where the observing instructor can shift D-rings and cinch straps to arrive at optimal trim. Once your rig is properly adjusted, it will be completely personalized. A diver with differing body morphology is as unlikely to fit in your harness as you are his. For this reason, it is rare that divers will use rental side mount rigs. Most instructors require divers to own their own kit, unless they are taking part in try-dive scenarios as a part of a purchasing decision.

It is important to get assistance from a qualified instructor in order to fine tune the fit of your harness. Small adjustments can make the difference between comfort and frustration.

CONFIGURATION

CHAPTER

5

Equipment Placement

After harness selection and adjustment is completed, the diver is then faced with the question of how to stow the assortment of regulators, reels, lights, slates, etc. in a fashion that will be the most streamlined, reducing the chance for snags and entanglements. There is no standard method of carrying accessory equipment for side mount diving. Various harnesses may offer differing solutions. The following section will explore a range of options that are popular among side mount divers today. Each item will be discussed separately.

Cylinders

Proper placement of cylinders is the single most important aspect of the side mount system. If cylinders are not properly placed, the diver must contend with poor buoyancy and trim, as well as snag points and inefficient movement through the water. Poor trim increases a diver's breathing rate, and snag points may damage the cave.

Tanks are held in place in several different ways. In most cases, thick bungee cords run from behind the diver's back and under the arm to hold the valve end of the cylinders in place near the diver's armpit. These bungees are adjusted to hold the cylinders in a horizontal position on the diver while swimming.

Lamar Hires demonstrates an air sharing position. HIs tanks are mounted on ring-bungees, which support the weight of the cylinder on a hard fixed point.

The lower tanks attachment point of the cylinder will vary from diver to diver in order to fit the particular cylinders to the diver's torso height.

38

The lower attachment point is generally a brass or stainless steel clip or carabiner that is secured to the cylinder with a webbed band (such as a cam band) or metal band (such as a large stainless steel hose clamp) mounted on the cylinder at the midpoint or slightly lower, depending on the diver's body type.

Taller divers often set the clip near the bottom of the cylinder, while shorter-bodied persons secure the clip to the tank a little higher up on the cylinder. With shorter torsos, women tend to mount clips higher than men. The cylinder clip creates the pivot point of balance for the entire system. If the diver is "foot heavy," then placing the cylinder clip lower will make the cylinder tip further toward the diver's head giving the diver a more head-down position. If the diver's feet tend to rise in the water, then shifting the clip higher on the cylinder will help drop the feet for more horizontal trim.

Wes Skiles demonstrates how tanks will hang parallel to the diver's body using a choker system.

In this rig, bungees are pulled around tank valves without the necessity for a choker system.

A closeup view of a tank choker system.

The clip or carabiner is then attached to the harness near the diver's hip or rear end, allowing for a secure, but easily removable connection.

A properly adjusted cylinder should ride parallel to the diver's body with the valve protected by the diver's arms, just below the armpit. The protection afforded to the valve connection in the side mount configuration is one of the system's greatest benefits, though there are several others:

One benefit of using cam bands to secure the lower tank attachment point is that there will be no need to bring tools for adjusting bands during travel or in the water. Cam bands can also allow for quick conversion to single tank diving.

1. It allows easy access to the valve handles in the event of a free flowing or damaged regulator. Some divers argue that tank valves should be turned "off" when not in use. But, leaving the unused cylinder in the "on" position allows for immediate access to a secondary air supply. This method is commonly used by side mount divers. On the other hand, this leaves the pressurized regulator vulnerable to free flow as the diver maneuvers through tight restrictions. Additionally, a diver using a scooter might have difficulty reaching the valve to secure a gas system failure. Disabling the air supply each time the regulator is switched increases task loading and is time consuming. The diver must decide whether the time and task loading involved with the continual securing of cylinder valves outweighs the chances of losing gas in a free flow situation.

2. The elimination of a crossover valve with this type of system creates an independent cylinder configuration. Gas loss in one cylinder is restricted to that cylinder without having to secure an isolation valve.

Valves and regs must be accessible with either hand.

3. The crossover/isolation valve that makes back mounted cylinders safe/redundant is also the most vulnerable part of the gas supply system, especially in overhead environments. These valves are the most likely failure point during an impact with the ceiling.

Donning tanks with ringed-bungees

If you are diving from a boat or hiking through the jungle, there may be times when you need to walk with tanks or don them topside. Using ring bungees, Lamar Hires demonstrates the steps necessary to safely secure tanks. All weight is borne by hard attachments, rather than bungees.

Donning tanks underwater

It is even easier to don tanks in the water. In some cases the upper attachment is clipped first and then the lower attachment is swung into position. In other cases, the lower attachment is clipped first. In both situations, the diver must be careful to protect the environment around him/her when swinging tanks into position.

41

Clipping a regulator second stage to a shoulder D-ring. The long hose is wrapped behind the diver's neck and is equipped with a fixed elbow to reduce jaw fatigue.

Although not required, it is highly recommended that side mount regulators use a DIN type connection over the standard yoke type. The DIN connection is more robust and is less prone to line snags or becoming unseated in the event of impact (although this is less likely in side mount). The only drawback to this type of connection is that it is more difficult to remove and replace first stages on cylinders in underwater emergencies should such a catastrophic, life-threatening out-of-gas situation occur. Regulator first stages should both be the same (i.e. both DIN or both yoke) so that emergency replacement can be conducted. It should be noted that if this type of extreme maneuver is ever used, the regulators must be completely rebuilt by a certified technician prior to the next dive.

Second stage regulators are either clipped to the harness high on the chest or secured from neck loops when not in use. There are a few manufacturers whose second stages are designed to receive the low pressure hose from either the right or left hand side. These types, and "no-handed" (neither right nor left-handed) second stage regulators such as

Wes Skiles using a neck bungee to stow second stages. The ninety-degree hard swivel reduces jaw fatigue.

some side exhaust models can make hose routing more streamlined.

The diver also has the option to either criss-cross the hoses behind the neck (one left handed second stage is required for this), run two short hoses in front from both the left and right, or run a long hose from one side, to criss-cross over the diver's neck to the opposite side. Hose routing is more mission specific than anything else. Divers who dive

in mixed teams with back mount divers, or instructors diving in training dives while in the side mount configuration, must use a long hose for gas sharing capability.

Another option that can make hose routing more streamlined is the use of angle adapters at the second stage. These adapters contain "captured" O-Rings that enable the second stage to swivel easily, allowing the hose to lay flatter to the diver's body,

The short high pressure hose directs the SPG toward the diver's field of vision. In the upper photo, the inflator comes over the diver's left shoulder in a traditional fashion.

The long hose may be routed from a left tank around the back of the diver's neck. The inflator in the lower photo is attached to the traditional position for a butt dump valve, but the top of the inflator is still secured in an accessible position, high on the chest.

43

Side Mount Cave Instructor Richard Dreher uses two long hoses to increase safety and reduce jaw fatigue associated with some short hose configurations.

Line arrows have been integrated into the hand mount.

but are not considered a weak link in the breathing system like other after-market swivels. The use of spherical rotating swivels is discouraged since some have failed during dives when the O-Ring extruded between the two half-round sections of the swivel, creating a massive loss of gas, and rendering that cylinder unusable.

If standard second stage regulators are used, a longer hose may be required on the left cylinder to accommodate rotating the second stage into the diver's mouth. Short LP hoses are roughly 26 inches long.

BCD inflator hoses are usually very short and routed under the arm or through the harness from the left cylinder.

High pressure gauge hoses are typically short, 6-inch types, arranged on the regulator to stay near the diver's chest. The gauges can also be attached to short bungees, on the diver's chest, keeping them pulled up out of the way. Some divers point the gauges upward and others run them down along the tank.

Lights

In the last decade, primary canister lights have changed more than any other piece of cave diving equipment. Smaller, more powerful and longer lasting HID and LED bulbs have given cave divers light sources that can handle both depth and abuse without having to take into consideration changes in trim or snag issues as was the case with larger battery canisters.

Mounting primary light canisters on the diver's harness is generally accomplished by either butt or waist mounting.

BUTT MOUNTING

Butt mounting the canister across the diver's rear end, while running the cable up through the harness, reduces snag potential and will keep the canister from being damaged in tight spaces.

One great advantage to butt mounting the battery pack is that it allows easy removal while underwater in a confined space. If the light cord or canister catches, one or both of the attachment points can be undone, allowing the diver to pass the snag and reattach the canister by feel. This is a skill that must be practiced and should be included in any side mount diver course. The use of easy to open brass or stainless steel clips or elastic bands is highly recommended for attaching the canister to the diver.

Butt mounting a canister light usually requires a longer length of cable than is found on most manufacturers' standard models. However most manufacturers will custom fit your light with a longer length of cable at the time of purchase or even as an add-on service with older models. Adding longer cable to your canister light yourself will usually void any warranty offered by the manufacturer, so it's a good idea to have them do it for you and pressure test it at the facility.

A butt mounted canister light can be very low profile. It can be secured to the rear attachments or may be slung lower under the crotch strap, which will allow it to rest underneath the curve of the buttocks.

TRADITIONAL WAIST MOUNT

The small size of the latest battery canisters allows them to be placed on the waist belt and ride either under or over the cylinder without being uncomfortable or creating a snag hazard. The waist strap attachment can also be set up for quick release in case of obstruction. Dive Rite Manufacturing makes an elastic quick-mount, specifically to facilitate easy removal of the waist mounted light canister in a small passage or restriction.

In both butt mount and waist mount configurations, the light head itself is carried in the hand, at-

A canister, mounted on top of the wing, may become problematic in small areas.

Some primary lights are operated without an auxiliary battery pack (left). A traditional waist mounted canister light (right).

tached to a hand mount, clipped off to the harness or attached to a helmet.

FLASHLIGHT MODELS

Small, powerful hand held "flashlight" style HID and LED primary lights alleviate the need to manage a canister and cable. Longer burn times and greater lumens improve new designs, and these lights are quickly gaining popularity as an alternative to canister-style lights. These lights are not yet as powerful as canister lights, and in larger rooms or passages can seem inadequate, but as the designs and power are improved, they will likely become the light of choice for many side mount divers.

Flashlight style lights should have some sort of lanyard system attached to the light and clipped to the diver's harness in case the light is dropped. The lanyard should permit the diver to fully extend their arm, or allow helmet mounting of the light, but not be so long as to create an entanglement or snag hazard.

BACKUP LIGHTS

Backup lights used by side mount divers are usually very small, and can be stowed and reached easily. LED technology has nearly taken over the

Handheld lights may also be stowed on a helmet to allow for surveying or hands-free operation.

small waterproof light market, offering much longer burn times for the amount of energy used. Many divers attach the lights to the harness or stow them in a pocket or in a pouch that allows for easy access. Other divers mount these lights on a helmet for accessibility in a lights out/ low visibility scenario, as well as providing illumination when both hands are used for work such as surveying or research.

Turning on a helmet mounted backup light.

A backup light secured at a high point on the harness will be easy to reach in confined spaces.

Reels

Exploration, safety and gap reels seem to snag more than anything else. Small reels can be mounted high on the chest, but can snag while in low bedding planes. Reels can also be mounted on D-rings on the diver's waist behind the cylinders. These items must be equipped with clips that can be easily undone. Newer side-winder style reels create less of a snag hazard due to their smaller frames and closer tolerances between the frame and the reel spool.

Reels may be secured to rear waist D-rings, if you are able to reach them. This keeps tank rails free of clutter.

Reels stowed on the center rear D-ring.

A knife stored under the epaulette is easy to reach.

Jerry Murphy stows a small Z-knife on the wrist strap of his computer for easy access.

Choosing finger spools (small reels without frames or knobs) further reduces the likelihood of snags and jams.

Knives and Computers

These items usually end up on the diver's forearm or high on the chest. Some divers use plastic parachute cord cutters, but these often rust, and must be cleaned and lubricated after every dive. Very small titanium knives are quickly becoming the cutting device of choice since they require no maintenance and hold a good, sharp edge. Knives can also be placed in a removable pouch, sometimes referred to as a "man purse." This pouch is used for various items such as knives, slates, backup masks, decompression tables, spare clips etc. and are usually mounted to the diver by a clip that allows it to hang from the diver's waist but above the cylinder. These pouches usually lie flat in the gap between the diver's tank and thigh and rarely snag.

Dive computers are almost always attached to the forearm for ease of reading and protection. Lens guards are a necessity. Backup dive computers can be worn in tandem with the primary, worn on the opposite wrist, or placed in a pocket or pouch. Remember that during gas switches the backup computer must be switched to the appropriate gases throughout the dive at the same time as the primary.

The Access Zone

When diving in small caves, consideration must be given to the placement of critical gear. Anything above the nipple line is considered accessible, where items placed lower on the body may be difficult or impossible to reach. A small knife on the waist belt may be impractical to reach, yet a knife attached to the computer wrist or chest strap may be easier. Further-

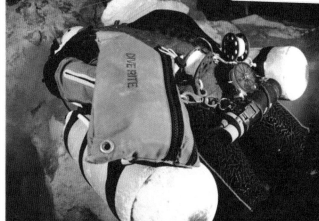

Items in the access zone above the nipple line may be reached with either hand.

Many items can be properly stowed on the diver's butt plate. When each item has its own attachment point, accessories are easy to locate and manage.

If you carry a lot of accessory equipment, such as survey gear, a "man purse" may provide the easiest and most accessible solution.

Russian instructor Evgeniy Runkov uses lead weights on his harness to adjust his trim while diving in the cold water of Ordinskaya Cave.

Australian instructor Linda Claridge finds the proper center of balance on small tanks.

more, some equipment should be accessible with either hand. Prior to your dive or prior to reaching a choke point in the cave, envision what could happen if you became stuck. Can you dump air from your wing? Can you reach the alternate regulator with either hand? Is your knife accessible if entanglement occurs?

Underwater

BUOYANCY AND TRIM

While underwater, the side mount rig will eventually change its point of balance due to the use of the gas in each cylinder. As the pivot point of balance changes (usually just below the shoulder blades), the arrangement of positively and negatively buoyant accessories can be rearranged. Some divers choose to frequently change between the right and left gas supplies during the dive, in order to keep the balance of the rig even. This works well, especially with cylinders that tend to get "light" as more of the gas is used. The buoyancy characteristics of some steel cylinders do not change as rapidly during the dive, often making these a better choice for side mounting.

Reels, lights, stage cylinders and other accessories can also be moved around during the dive in order to fine tune buoyancy. Some drysuit users find that they can achieve better buoyancy control with their suit, and only use the BCD jacket or air cell as a backup. Experimentation (preferably not in a silty cave) is the best way to fine tune your side mount system.

CCR Side Mount

Perhaps the newest facet of side mount diving is represented by a small contingent of divers who are adapting their rebreathers for side mount diving. In one configuration, the diver wears a side mounted rebreather with an oxygen sphere on one side, and a large diluent supply bottle on the other side. Still others are experimenting with dual, side mounted rebreathers. In this case, the diver wears a rebreather canister with oxygen sphere and diluent bottle on each side of their body. Some of the greatest challenges with this configuration come from getting the breathing loop situated for comfort and functionality. Pendulum hose and valve configurations may be a cleaner solution for these types of units as they are refined in the future.

Exploration potential for a dual, side mounted CCR is significant. The range of such a device may offer substantial time for patient exploration without the pressure of a dwindling gas supply. However, small cave passages may present a greater risk to these divers. A CCR has many more delicate aspects that are not conducive to grinding and bumping in small cave. The gas dynamics of removal and replacement may be more challenging than just a SCUBA tank.

At the time of this writing, these types of devices were only available in kit form, placing the liability in the hands of the diver that assembles the parts. Modification of any standard rebreather bears significant risk. Third party testing will not have anticipated the types of unique changes that you make to a unit. Home builders should be very cautious, realizing that they are placing their chances for survival on an experiment that may have fatal consequences.

Cave diving scientist Dr. Tom Iliffe uses a chest mounted pouch to carry delicate specimens.

Right: Curt Bowen prepares to make a quick dive into a new cave in the Dominican Republic, using his Armadillo rig, equipped with a climbing harness.

A mixed team of Russian cave divers.

GAS
MANAGEMENT

CHAPTER

6

Basic Principles

One of the greatest benefits of side mounted, independent cylinders, is the ability to self-manage gas emergencies. Both regulators and valves are easily visible to detect leaks or shut down in a gas loss situation. The use of the thirds rule (one third of the gas supply is used during the inward penetration of the dive, and two thirds of the total gas supply is saved for exit and emergencies) applies to gas management, and is just as important for side mount diving as it is with back mount cave diving. Due to the increased task loading associated with switching second stage regulators, the diver must remember that both cylinder gauges must be monitored more frequently than if manifolded doubles were being used.

Whether diving alone or with a buddy, a side mount diver should be capable of independent management of gas supply emergencies. Side mounters often find themselves in low visibility or tight spaces and must be capable of self rescue.

The rate at which regulator switches are conducted is often debated by side mount divers, depending on their experiences. Students are generally instructed to conduct regulator exchanges every 200 to 300 psi (15 – 20 bar) from each cylinder. This establishes a rhythm and muscle memory that is required for efficient exchanges, regulator recoveries, gauge monitoring and proper buoyancy and trim when cylinder buoyancy characteristics change throughout the dive.

The frequent (200 to 300 psi) switching between gas supplies also ensures that in the event of a gas sharing scenario, or free flow in one of the side mount diver's primary cylinders, the diver has adequate reserve available in the "good" cylinder for dealing with emergencies.

Gas Supply Malfunctions

If one of the side mounted cylinders develops a malfunction, the diver has two basic responses to accomplish self rescue:

NO GAS AVAILABLE FROM THE CYLINDER:
- Immediately switch to the working regulator and establish visual contact with the guideline and buddy, if team diving.
- Close and then re-open the supply valve of the compromised cylinder to confirm that it is not delivering gas (possible roll-off).

- Signal buddy (if team diving), call the dive, and both divers abort, with the compromised diver leading out of the cave/wreck and the other diver retaining close visual contact. The compromised diver will breathe from the good cylinder until either the entrance or decompression gas supply is reached.
- In the event that the gas supply in the good cylinder drops to low levels and there is a dive buddy, the dive buddy will commence gas sharing until the entrance or decompression gases are reached. The compromised diver should not completely drain a tank prior to initiating a gas sharing scenario. More options for survival are available when even small gas supplies remain in more than one tank.

GAS AVAILABLE, BUT SECOND STAGE IS FREE FLOWING:
- Immediately shut down the free flowing regulator and switch to the good cylinder.
- Establish visual contact with the guideline and dive buddy if team diving.
- Re-open supply valve on compromised cylinder to confirm that there is still a problem.

Deploying a long hose to another diver is similar to back mount technique when the hose is wrapped behind the diver's head.

- While swimming out of the cave, begin "feathering" the valve (partially open and then close with each breath) and breathe off of it until the entrance or decompression gases are reached or until gas supply in that cylinder is depleted.
- Switch to good cylinder once compromised cylinder is depleted and continue to the exit or decompression gas supply.
- If gas in both cylinders drops low during exit, and team diving, then switch to air sharing scenario until the entrance or decompression gases are reached.

Gas Sharing Techniques

When discussing gas sharing contingencies, it should be noted that the best possible scenario for efficient egress from water is via self rescue. The diver should use most of their available, self-carried gas sources before resorting to sharing gas with another diver. In all configurations, the diver should attempt to breathe a damaged regulator first by feathering the valve, then switch to the functioning cylinder or stage tanks, then as a last resort, gas sharing with another diver if team diving.

Discussion often arises about removing one side mounted cylinder in an out of gas emergency. Donation of one complete gas system has serious implications to the team and the removal of a cylinder can place the donor in a hazardous situation. Buoyancy and weight are planned around retaining both tanks for ballast. Swapping cylinders can be time consuming and donating one for the entire duration of the exit can slow the team dramatically due to poor trim and buoyancy.

Exploration side mount diving requires a true solo mentality. Team members may be available to assist each other with restrictions and line entanglements, yet gas sharing could easily lead to a double fatality. Dive planning for self rescue is imperative.

There are two schools of thought on how to share gas while wearing a side mount configuration. The first group feels that side mount should only be used for exploration style diving and that the diver should be independent, with self rescue being the only option in a gas loss emergency. These divers are unlikely to utilize a long hose for gas sharing.

The second group believes that the side mount configuration is not necessarily an exploration-specific configuration. As a result, a means of emergency gas sharing (long hose) is included in their kit. Instructors or dive guides who are responsible for the safety of students or clients must include a long hose in their gear.

There are two variations on gas sharing. Depending on how the diver(s) and cave are configured, one will work better than the other.

Sharing with a Long Hose

Air sharing positions vary depending on diver configurations and whether you are open water, wreck or cave diving. If the passage in a cave or wreck will allow, and the donating diver is rigged with a long hose, then the compromised diver will swim alongside and slightly in front of the donor so that the compromised diver and breathing source is in full view and in contact with the donor. The compromised diver should always have one hand on the donated hose to ensure that it will not be pulled from their mouth during egress.

In some cases, stage tank removal may be the best solution for gas sharing, especially when the team must pass through a restriction. A stage bottle may be fully used and discarded in an emergency, but the primary tanks worn by the diver should not be removed for donation.

Passing through restrictions requires additional time on exit, when visibility has been destroyed. It is important to maintain a relaxed breathing rate, even in the face of emergency.

If a restricted area of a cave or wreck is encountered during exit, then the compromised diver takes the lead in a classic single file formation and the donor follows as closely behind as possible using both diver and line contact. It is assumed that visibility will be decreased within restricted areas, therefore maintaining contact should be a priority.

Using Short Hoses

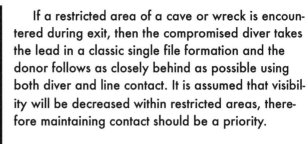

When team divers are both configured with short hoses on each cylinder, then an "over and under" profile can be taken with the compromised diver on the bottom, and the donor holding on to the shoulders and swimming above the compromised diver. One of the regulators is lowered down to the compromised diver from above and the team swims toward the entrance as long as the cave or wreck configuration will allow.

A mixed team consists of a combination of back mount, CCR and/or side mount divers. Diving in a mixed team requires additional planning and rehearsal of gas management and emergency procedures.

If the team plans on traversing multiple or long restrictions, the compromised diver should ask for donated gas early, before supplies are expended. If some gas is saved in their own cylinder(s), then it can be used to transit the restricted areas, where the donor will not be able to take the over and under position. Once the cave allows for sharing gas again, the over and under position can be reestablished.

Additional Considerations

CONSERVATIVE PLANNING

As with all cave dives, there are times when divers should plan more conservative gas reserves, such as diving in new caves, diving with new partners, using new equipment, and entering in siphoning water flow or uncertain tides. There are also instances specific to side mount diving that warrant a more conservative approach to gas management, including:

LOSS OF VISIBILITY

The loss of visibility due to silting is more common while diving in the smaller passages of the side mount cave. Low visibility will drastically slow a diver's exit, therefore conservative reserves will ensure that a diver will have sufficient gas to deal with an increase in bottom time due to a low visibility exit.

SNAGS AND RESTRICTIONS

Side mount divers can spend much more time and gas negotiating restrictions on the exit portion of the dive, either due to the physical orientation of the restrictions, or to the fact that these restrictions will be more challenging in low to zero visibility caused by the silt that results from the inbound portion of the dive. Gas planning for various cave and wreck diving circumstances should be a part of a comprehensive risk assessment before the dive, and should remain very flexible for unforeseen obstacles encountered during the dive. Divers must keep in mind that slowing their breathing rate while transiting though restricted areas will conserve gas as well as lower their physical profile within the restriction. Even greater gas reserves should be considered when the chances of exiting a restricted cave or wreck are compounded by low visibility.

Mixed Teams

Although side mount divers are effectively self sufficient in gas management, due to the independent cylinder configuration, there are instances where they dive in a mixed team with back mount and/or CCR divers. Prior to diving, you may need to reconfigure your gear for air sharing and should agree on emergency management scenarios prior to getting in the water. In almost all cases, long hoses are used. During your in-water safety drill, you should rehearse gas sharing.

Gas Management in a Nutshell

1. Plan Your Dive: Consider conditions that might demand a more conservative gas plan (restrictions, low visibility, solo, new gear, new buddy, tides, siphons, etc.).

2. Practice: Rehearse gas supply emergencies during your in-water safety check.

3. Stay in Balance: Swap regulators often to ensure proper function and to maintain horizontal trim. Remain mentally balanced with good control over breathing.

4. Be Conservative: At all times, a diver should be capable of self rescue and capable of buddy rescue.

OPEN WATER
SIDE MOUNT

CHAPTER 7

Open Water Side Mount Diver

Overview

The Open Water Side Mount Diver Course presents techniques that are commonly used for diving double independent cylinders in open water diving scenarios. These techniques include:

- Shore diving
- Offshore diving from small and large boats
- Single and double cylinder removals at the surface and underwater
- Mixed teams concept – back mount and side mount buddy teams
- Foundations for technical diving

The Purpose of Side Mount Configuration in Open Water Diving

Recreational divers have been using single cylinders to explore the underwater realm since the 1940s. Although equipment has been refined over the years, the essential diving configuration has changed very little. Redundant octopus regulators and inflatable buoyancy devices improved safety, yet true redundancy was only found by divers carrying back mounted double tanks.

In recent years, media attention covering the work of cave explorers has brought side mount configuration into popular view. Recreational divers who were preparing to move into the next phase of their education wondered why they could not utilize the same techniques as cave explorers to improve the safety and redundancy of their diving rigs.

Over the years, disagreements ensued regarding which doubles configuration could be deemed the safest option. Double independent back mounts, manifolded doubles and isolator manifolds each claimed their place as the safest configuration. Recently, re-evaluating independent tanks, divers also revisited the question of diving side mount in open water. With the availability of off-the-shelf units on the rise and the development of open water curricula, it seems this configuration is experiencing the greatest growth in diving systems today.

An open water side mount course will cover offshore diving techniques for small and large boats.

62

Some of the benefits for open water divers include:

- Improved gas supply redundancy over single tank diving
- Easier access and monitoring of tank valves and regulators
- Easier access to single tanks while traveling
- Improved trim and streamlining
- Easy to secure tanks on hang lines under boats
- Lighter to carry one tank at a time to the boat or shore
- Greater range of motion of head and neck
- Greater peripheral vision
- No need to adjust "bands and bolts" on rental tanks when traveling
- Best possible fit for a wide range of body morphologies
- Ability to travel with one rig that can accommodate any type of recreational singles or doubles diving
- Divers with injuries or disabilities that prevented them from carrying heavy double cylinders on the surface are able to deal with cylinders one at a time and only carry the full weight while supported by the water.

For the wreck diving community, side mounted cylinders are giving divers access to areas of the wreck previously deemed too small for exploration by divers in back mounted doubles. Reef divers are able to negotiate smaller areas without damaging fragile coral formations and overall streamlining is improved for currents and flow.

Extended Range

With the addition of a second gas cylinder, a diver is often exposed to more extreme environmental and physiological factors than the recreational single-cylinder diver. These factors are:

- Increased bottom times.
- Increased depths and or distance from point of entry.

Side mount harnesses may not hold a diver in an upright position on the surface as well as an open water BCD. Off-the-shelf rigs are designed primarily to support horizontal trim underwater. Keeping the buoyancy low on the hips of the unit and out of the shoulder region gives a side mount diver the smallest profile and best trim.

- Increased exposure to water with the possibility of thermal issues.
- Increased decompression obligation (staged decompression) requiring decompression gas planning.
- Increased chance of equipment malfunction. The more time that equipment is put into the water, the greater the chance that some part will eventually fail.

When divers increase their ability to stay underwater for longer periods of time all of the above issues come into play and must be appropriately planned for. It cannot be stressed enough that once the diver carries an additional gas supply, it is very easy to move out of the realm of recreational diving and into technical diving. There are literally only minutes of bottom time differing between the two types of diving, but there can be hours of planning and set-up required to safely complete the latter.

Bungee cords alone may not be adequate to support the weight of a tank if you are walking or jumping off of a boat. The tank may need a hard, secure point for entry (below), which may be released after descent.

Cylinder Removal

The removal and replacement of one or both cylinders while on the surface or underwater is one of the key benefits to the side mount configuration. Though there should be very few scenarios when the open water side mount diver should have the need to remove any cylinder underwater, it may arise when cylinders must be donned or removed on the surface, while entering or exiting the water.

Removal and replacement of cylinders to access small areas of reef, caves or wrecks is considered overhead environment diving and requires specialized skills and training. Divers interested in this type of environment are required to seek out Side Mount Diver training from a certified and qualified Side Mount Diver Instructor specializing in overhead environments. Underwater cylinder removals are NOT recommended at this level of diving. The reasons for this are:

- Separation from ballast: As soon as a diver removes a cylinder, he or she must be prepared for the loss of ballast that prevents an uncontrolled ascent.

This can be catastrophic if any decompression obligation has been obtained during the dive.

- Separation from gas supply: In the same scenario, the diver stands to lose not only their ballast, but their entire gas supply if the cylinder is not tethered in a secure method.

When a cylinder is removed or donned on the surface, the diver should make every attempt to maintain control through the use of "hang lines" on the side of the vessel or through the use of "load lanyards," which provide a more sturdy connection of the cylinder valve to the diver than the standard bungee systems do. These items will be covered in the next chapter. Dropping a cylinder while on the surface during the donning or removal process will often result in the permanent loss of that cylinder, or possible injury to any divers diving below the vessel.

It is important to become proficient at tank removal and replacement in the water. This technique should be mastered in shallow water as well as from locations where you cannot touch bottom and must retrieve gear from an equipment line.

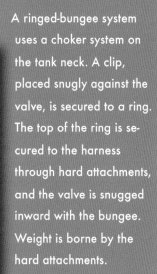

A ringed-bungee system uses a choker system on the tank neck. A clip, placed snugly against the valve, is secured to a ring. The top of the ring is secured to the harness through hard attachments, and the valve is snugged inward with the bungee. Weight is borne by the hard attachments.

Diving from Boats

Most divers realize that underwater the side mount configuration has great advantages over a back mounted set of double cylinders. However, on the surface or boat, the side mount diver can be at a disadvantage. Diver benches and ladders are not designed with the side mount diver in mind, and the wider profile of a side mount diver can be an issue on the crowded, rocking deck of a dive boat. There are several points that may help make your open water side mount diving trip easier on you and the crew of the vessel. First, talk to the Captain, Divemaster or Instructor on board and let them know about your needs as a side mount diver. Ask them if there is a certain area that they would like you to set up in, how to stow cylinders while underway, where and when they would like you to enter/exit the water and what assistance they might be willing to lend.

If you prefer to enter the water without cylinders and have them handed down to you one at a time, then the crew will need to know this well in advance and they may have you go into the water first (or last) in order to keep the dive deck/ladder clear for other divers. If sea conditions are rough or surface currents are strong, this may not be possible. Having the boat anchored or moored over the dive site in calm sea conditions may be one instance where this style of entry works well.

The use of "hang lines" over the side of a small dive boat works well if conditions (sea state and currents) allow. These short lines allow the diver to drop their cylinders over the side of the boat to be attached while floating on the surface. These lines allow the cylinders to hang about 1 foot below the surface, where they can easily be reached by a floating diver. When the diver returns from the dive, the cylinders

Work with the boat crew to install specialized gear such as hang lines. Let them know precisely what type of assistance you will require to safely enter and exit the water.

are detached and hung on the lines once again until the diver is on board and can pull them up. Charter boats are unlikely to have these types of lines available to you, so you should bring your own onboard.

By far, the most self-sufficient and stable method of securing side mounted cylinders for entry and exit involves the use of "load lanyards." These sturdy nylon line or webbing lanyards allow the cylinders to be clipped to the upper harness D-ring and can handle the full weight of the cylinder while the diver is entering or exiting the water. These devices take all the weight off of the side mount bungee system and are highly recommended for any open water side mount diver. Once the diver is in the water, load lanyards can be left in place or removed and clipped off to the harness somewhere or stowed in a pocket. Just prior to the diver coming back to the surface, the lanyards can be put back in place so the diver may come directly up and over the dive boat ladder just as their back mount counterparts do. Load lanyards are to be used in conjunction with the side mount bungee system, and are not intended to replace it all together. Although they offer stability, they bring the top of the tank forward and increase the horizontal profile of the diver.

Dive Rite offers a similar solution referred to as a "ringed-bungee system." This system uses stainless hardware to hook the top end of the bungee to the chest D-ring. The tank is clipped to a large stainless ring, and the load is held snug with the bungee, which is below the weight-bearing part of the system. Divers with this system can easily climb a boat ladder or walk with their tanks on without worry of a bungee snapping under load.

Open Water Safety

There are a few points that open water side mount divers need to keep in mind while using this configuration:
• Most side mount harnesses are not designed to float the diver in a head up position in an

HANG LINES: Remember to pull up all hang lines on both sides of the boat before getting underway. SCUBA cylinders can do a lot of damage to a boat if they are banging against the sides at high speed.

Load lanyard used on the cylinder neck.

emergency. Additional buoyancy (drysuit or dual bladder) or emergency buoyancy devices should be considered when diving in remote places, heavy currents or heavy seas.

• Some side mount harnesses now being sold do not come with a buoyancy control device. These systems are designed for cave divers or sump divers and should never be used in open water without a proper buoyancy control device being incorporated into the harness.

• Many open water divers are not familiar with the side mount configuration's safety and redundancy benefits. Open water side mount divers who dive with other conventionally configured divers should take the time to rehearse out-of-gas and other diving related emergencies.

Mixed Teams in Open Water

Although the redundancy provided by side mounted independent cylinders provides the diver with a greater chance of self rescue, there are several instances where the diver may be required to configure for a gas sharing situation:

• Open water side mount diving instructors who must provide air sharing capabilities for students in training.

Although you are diving in open water, it is still critical to trim tanks properly, bringing them parallel to your body. Poorly secured tanks damage the environment and leave you off balance.

Regardless of your team's individual configuration, you should rehearse air sharing scenarios prior to descent.

• Open water side mount divers who dive in mixed teams with back mount divers (in either singles or manifolded doubles) and must provide air sharing capabilities for the rest of the team.

• Open water side mount teams where each team member feels more comfortable having access to another source of air during the dive (triple redundancy).

There are a few ways that the open water side mount diver can provide air to another diver. The first is to use a 5- to 7-foot long hose on one of the cylinders. The excess hose can be run down the length of the cylinder and bungeed in place to prevent snag hazards. There are arguments for placing this long hose on either the right or the left cylinder, and it is up to the diver to decide

which is most comfortable and efficient for deployment in an emergency.

Gas sharing from a standard hose usually means the divers must ascend directly to the surface, often disregarding safety stops and potentially leaving them long distances from the surface vessel. Add surface currents and high seas, and an out-of-gas emergency underwater quickly turns into divers in distress on the surface.

Deploying a 5- to 7-foot hose during an out of gas emergency provides both divers with the space they need to swim efficiently back to the ascent/descent line as well as allowing them to conduct an efficient safety stop prior to surfacing.

When two divers must share gas at any great depth, such as on a deep wall or wreck, a single cylinder with an octopus can become insufficient to get both divers to the surface. The increased depth combined with the likelihood of an increased respiration rate can quickly overcome the flow design of the first stage regulator, creating a scenario where neither diver is being provided sufficient gas (over-breathing). This can lead to CO_2 buildup and possibly even unconsciousness in one or both divers.

With the independent cylinder design of the side mounted system, both divers essentially end up with their own gas supply and over-breathing is not an issue.

It is still possible to share air with another diver even if the side mount diver does not have a long

Side mount configuration is gaining popularity among divers who wish to protect their valves and regulators from damage caused in overhead environments. Additional technical training beyond an Open Water Side Mount Class is needed for diving in overhead environments of any type.

hose. If the open water side mount diver is the gas donor, he/she can get behind the out of gas diver, holding on to the other diver's valve. Either one of the side mount diver's short second stages can be deployed over the recipient's shoulder while both divers begin the ascent to the surface. This is not considered the most efficient technique in a gas sharing emergency, but it will work if done correctly.

The open water side mount diver should remember that removing and donating an entire side mount cylinder can leave him/her extremely unbalanced and lacking the appropriate ballast to maintain an efficient swimming position. Donating an entire cylinder in an out-of-gas emergency is not recommended. In summary, the most efficient method of sharing gas is through the use of a properly maintained and stowed long hose.

Entering into Technical Diving

With the addition of larger gas supplies (double cylinders), the open water side mount diver is generally entering into the realm of diving dubbed "Technical Diving," and will be exposed to several physical and psychological issues not encountered with single cylinder recreational diving.

Increased gas supplies equate directly to increased exposures (bottom times). Depending on depth and gas(es) used, this will probably place the diver either past or very close to the no decompression diving limits. Open water side mount divers should consider formal training in more advanced diving techniques such as Nitrox diving, Advanced Nitrox Diving, Staged Decompression Diving and Technical Diving. Any of these training courses will expose the diver to the protocols and techniques associated with technical dive planning that include:
• Decompression planning and techniques
• Emergency procedures
• Thermal considerations for extended bottom times

Even though open water side mount divers learn how to remove and replace tanks for emergencies, they are not ready to penetrate restrictions in wrecks and caves without additional specific technical training.

- Use of optimal breathing gases for particular diving depths and times
- Gas planning and gas management contingencies for team emergencies

Spatial Awareness and Drag

The addition of a second cylinder inevitably increases the diver's profile. It may take the diver some time to realize how wide they are both on the surface as well as underwater. Spatial awareness of the diver's height and width will come with time, but new open water side mount divers need to increase their awareness, especially while swimming around fragile coral reefs or outside of wrecks.

The diver's larger profile also increases drag. A diver should be prepared for additional swimming effort, especially if there are currents involved. A good pair of rigid fins can help move the diver through the water, but an appropriate level of physical fitness is the most useful prerequisite for dealing with the added effort of diving with two tanks.

Summary

The side mount diving configuration is an extremely versatile, safe and stable diving configuration for use in open water. However, there are decompression considerations, emergency gas sharing contingencies and thermal comfort issues that must be addressed before diving with this technical configuration. Diving from boats in the side mount configuration is both easy and fun, but the diver must make proper equipment and support arrangements prior to the dive. Remember that proper dive planning and physical fitness will make your side mount diving experience safe and enjoyable.

An open water side mount diver has entered the realm of technical diving. Larger gas supplies inevitably lead to longer bottom times. Decompression training and deep diving procedures must be mastered for safe use beyond recreational diving limits.

SIDE MOUNT
CAVE DIVING

CHAPTER

8

Side Mount Diver Course

Overview

The Side Mount Diver Course presents techniques and equipment that allow cave divers to access smaller passages and take advantage of the many unique aspects of the side mount configuration. These aspects include:

- Benefits and history of the side mount configuration for cave diving
- Safety aspects of independent cylinder configuration
- Single and double cylinder removals for confined space diving
- Gas planning
- Mixed teams with back mount and/or CCR divers

A Side Mount Cave Diver Specialty Course is intended for experienced cave divers who intend to delve into smaller, siltier conditions, yet the considerations for this type of diving are valuable for all side mount divers.

Purpose of Side Mount in Caves

Recreational divers have been using single cylinders to explore the underwater realm since the 1940s. These adventurous souls braved the unknown depths with equipment that would be considered frail and technically simple by today's standards.

In the late 1980s, a wave of technical divers began holding seminars and workshops in the US essentially bringing technical and decompression diving techniques into the mainstream. Many of the recreational SCUBA training agencies considered these divers the lunatic fringe, vehemently admonishing any such diving practices, while scuba equipment manufacturers sent out notices stating that if any of their equipment was used in such diving practices (mostly the use of Nitrox), then any and all warranties were null and void.

The diving industry has come a long way since then, and now virtually every recreational SCUBA training agency and equipment manufacturer has jumped on board, creating their own "Tech" courses, standards or equipment.

Diving configurations within the technical diving community also evolved, with cave divers leading the way with innovations such as buoyancy devices, octopus regulators and double cylinders joined together with a single manifold, known then as the "Benjamin Crossover Valve." Dr. George Benjamin designed this manifold to facilitate his exploration into the deep blue holes of the Bahamas. His manifold became the standard for cave divers in many parts of the world.

True to their innovative roots, it was cave divers who first began configuring cylinders on their sides in order to gain access to small crevices within the dark passages that they explored. It would be 20 years or more before side mounted cylinders would gain recognition as a safe and stable alternative to hauling heavy manifolded double cylinders.

The trend toward this "new" configuration has had many catalysts within the diving industry, but here are a few that have brought side mount diving into the cave diving mainstream:

- Allows access to underwater passages that were deemed "too small" to enter with back mounted cylinders
- Truly independent, redundant gas supply, thus increased safety
- Ability to break down the doubles "package" into two separate, and more manageable, packages
- Enables divers with injuries or disabilities that prevented them from carrying heavy double cylinders, to deal with cylinders one at a time and only carry the full weight while supported by the water
- Enables divers to physically see and manipulate their SCUBA valve attachments during rare equipment malfunctions
- Allows for gas sharing contingencies
- Offers stability and streamlining comparable to, or better than double back mounted cylinders.

Historic Small Hope Bay Lodge in Andros was a favorite destination for cave explorer Dr. George Benjamin who developed the Benjamin Crossover Manifold. Ironically, today most cave exploration in Andros is done using side mount and rebreather configurations.

Equipment

Proper fit, adjustment and cylinder placement on a well-designed side mount harness are the core ingredients of any good system. The student is encouraged to seek out a certified and qualified side mount cave diving instructor who can assist with equipment purchasing decisions, equipment fit and configuration as well as formal training in side mount techniques for cave diving.

Harnesses

As illustrated in previous chapters of this book, there are many harness choices for the prospective side mount diver. Each harness has its strong and weak points. You should consider the type of diving you anticipate doing, such as:

• Small caves or side mount caves (some harnesses are more streamlined than others)
• Extended penetrations/stage diving
• Body size (some harnesses do not accommodate all body shapes and sizes)
• Drysuit or wetsuit use (back up buoyancy device)
• Cylinder size (possible lift issues with some harnesses and larger steel tanks)

Cylinders

Proper placement of cylinders is the single most important aspect of the side mount system. If the cylinders roll forward, or tilt up or down, there is an increased chance of snagging and drag. Most systems use thick bungee cords that cross over the diver's back to hold the valve end of the cylinders in place, while

older systems used bicycle inner tubes laced through the harness. Both can be adjusted to keep the cylinders in a horizontal position on the diver while swimming. The second attachment point is usually a web or metal band affixed with a clip or carabiner and mounted on the cylinder at the mid section or a bit lower depending on the diver's body type and harness design. The clip or carabiner is then attached to the harness near the diver's hip or rear end, allowing for a secure, but easily removable connection.

Cylinders should sit horizontally on the diver's sides. The valve position may be as far forward as the diver's armpits, or as far back as the diver's pectoral muscles, depending on the diver's body type and cylinder type. Valve handles are much more protected from projections and roll-offs in these positions and also allow for per-breath "feathering" of the valve in a free flowing regulator scenario (something nearly impossible to do efficiently with a manifold).

One of the greatest safety attributes of the independent cylinder configuration is that gas loss from one cylinder does not affect gas in the other cylinder. This huge safety factor saves precious gas that would have been lost while trying to close the isolation valve on a back mounted manifold doubles system. Cross over/isolation valves that make back mounted cylinders safe/redundant are also the most vulnerable part of the doubles gas supply system, and usually the first thing to come into contact with the cave ceiling.

Valve and cylinder maintenance on side mount cylinders is paramount. Burst discs should be changed often and valve-to-cylinder o-rings should be changed at least every 6 months. Valve hand-

A good side mount diver can look at an opening in three dimensions and change the physical orientation of their body to best fit through small spaces. Ensuring that your cylinders stay stable during these rotations is important.

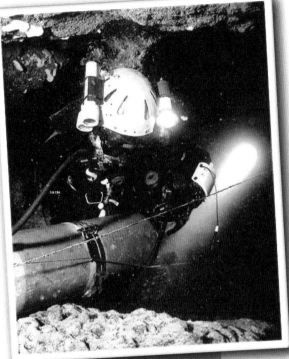

The constant grinding on equipment can be very hard on side mount gear. A diver must remain vigilant with maintenance.

Bill Rennaker points out potential locations for snags.

wheel nuts should be checked regularly since they become loose over time. As with all overhead diving, the side mount diver should remember that he/she is carrying a very finite amount of gas and separation from or loss of this gas may be fatal.

Side mount cylinders should be matched with equal weight and capacity to allow for proper trim in the water. Left and right handed "mirrored" valves, such as the ones taken from a dismantled and plugged manifold, are by far the favorite of side mount divers. These paired valves allow the cylinders, regulators and valve handles to be matched perfectly for attachment and access.

Appropriate cylinder sizes for side mount systems vary, and low pressure steel 85 cubic foot cylinders are a favorite in many areas. These cylinders have great trim, weight and capacity but they are not the best tool for the job in all cases. Cylinders with capacities over 100 cubic feet are often used by divers wishing to make greater penetrations, or for those with higher breathing rates. In Mexico many side mount divers use aluminum 80 cubic foot cylinders (11 liters), since they are readily available in the region. The shallow caves of Mexico lend well to the use of these cylinders and most side mount divers have placed additional D-rings on the waist band of their harnesses that permit the bottom of the cylinder to be clipped lower on the torso after the cylinder becomes light during the dive. There are many variations of this modification and your side mount instructor will be able to elaborate should you decide to dive with aluminum cylinders.

Regulators and Hoses

DIN-type connections are more robust and less prone to becoming unseated in the event of impact and are therefore the preferred choice of side mount cave divers. The only drawback to this type of connection is that it is more difficult to remove and replace first stages on cylinders in underwater emergencies. Although swapping regulators is time consuming and can increase exit time, it can allow a diver to take full advantage of remaining gas supplies in an otherwise disabled tank.

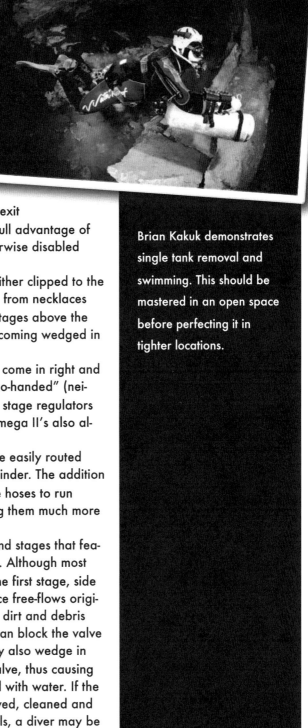

Brian Kakuk demonstrates single tank removal and swimming. This should be mastered in an open space before perfecting it in tighter locations.

Second stage regulators are either clipped to the harness high on the chest or hung from necklaces when not in use. Storing second stages above the nipple line prevents them from becoming wedged in low restrictions.

Some second stage regulators come in right and left-handed models while other "no-handed" (neither right nor left-handed) second stage regulators such as Poseidon and Oceanic Omega II's also allow for easy, ambidextrous use.

Standard second stages can be easily routed with longer hoses from the left cylinder. The addition of a hard-angle adapter allow the hoses to run tighter to the diver's body, making them much more snag resistant.

Some divers prefer using second stages that feature easily removable face covers. Although most regulator free-flows originate in the first stage, side mount divers sometimes experience free-flows originating in the second stage. When dirt and debris gets into a second stage body it can block the valve open causing a free-flow. Dirt may also wedge in between the body and exhaust valve, thus causing the second stage to continually fill with water. If the face cover can be carefully removed, cleaned and replaced without the need for tools, a diver may be able to recover an otherwise unusable regulator.

First stages that feature rotating low-pressure port turrets with multiple ports allow the LP hose to run in a user-friendly configuration. Some first stages also feature ports on the base of the low-pressure swivel turret, and these can be a great advantage for side mount hose routing.

Inflator hoses are usually very short and routed under the arm or through the harness from the left cylinder. The inflator button should be clipped high on the middle of the chest to keep it snag-free and accessible with either hand. In some cases these can be mounted in such a way that air can be released by bumping the button with the diver's chin which can be of great value if caught in a restriction.

High pressure gauge hoses are typically short, 6- to 9-inch types, arranged on the cylinder to stay upright, near the diver's chest or along the sides of the cylinder depending on the diver's preference. Both positions have advantages depending on the diver's body type and visual acuity. Divers with weaker vision may find that longer hoses allow them to keep the gauge at the proper reading distance, but they must be configured to be snag free.

Practice locating and unclipping each piece of equipment in a large open area. If you ever get lodged in a restriction you will be able to find the offending gear and release it from the cave's grasp.

Single and Double Cylinder Removals for Restrictions

While the side mount configuration itself allows the diver to move through smaller areas than their back mounting counterparts, the design of today's side mount harnesses allows us to easily remove one or both cylinders to access even smaller restrictions.

There are two key hazards that must be kept in mind when conducting cylinder removals:

- Separation from ballast: As soon as a diver removes a cylinder, he or she must be prepared for the loss of ballast that is keeping them from floating to the ceiling of the cave. This can be catastrophic if the cylinders are removed in a large room or fissure crack, prior to a restriction. If both cylinders must be removed it is highly recommended that at least one of the cylinders (the cylinder being breathed from) be tethered to the diver by a bungee or cord that is shorter than the length of the second stage hose on that cylinder.

- Separation from gas supply: In the same scenario as above, the diver stands to lose not only their ballast, but their entire gas supply if the cylinder is not tethered in a secure method.

When a cylinder is removed, the diver should make every attempt to maintain control either by tether or by hand-holding and pushing it in front of them. Some odd restriction configurations demand that one or the other cylinder be removed. If the restriction is angled upward or downward, then the diver should remove the cylinder that would be considered the "bottom" cylinder. The top cylinder will remain close to the diver's body simply through gravity, whereas the bottom cylinder would "hang" slightly below the diver increasing their profile and possibly snagging while passing the restriction.

Before passing any narrow restriction the diver should assess the following:

- Gas available for passing the restriction and further penetration; i.e. is it worth the effort of passing the restriction?
- Size-up the restriction. Is it passable in your current configuration or do you need to adapt? Do you need to drain air from the BCD, remove one or both tanks, come back with no-mount, etc.?
- If in a team, will all members be able to traverse the restriction and beyond before hitting their planned turn pressures?
- Will visibility allow for the entire team to efficiently pass the restriction after the first diver passes, especially when cylinder removals are required?

Once on the far side of the restriction, the diver should assess the return route for "one-way" snags to ensure that he/she will be able to pass the restriction without delay once the dive has been called

In exploration side mount diving, it may take a team to get you to the water, but once on site, solo diving may be a safe choice. The decision to solo dive may be based on conditions that include: passage configuration and size, silt, experience, contingency planning and availability of safety divers.

and ensure that both gas supply and visibility will be sufficient.

The entire return trip will be slowed significantly when multiple restrictions are passed by a team of side mount divers. Gas planning should take into consideration this very slow return to the exit.

Gas Planning

Gas planning for side mount cave diving must be conservative. Maximum penetration on two side mounted cylinders should be no more than one third of the gas supply carried (i.e. one third of the gas used for the inward portion of the dive, one third of the gas used for the swim out, and one third kept in reserve).

The side mount configuration allows divers to access smaller and often silty and muddy passages in the cave. This inevitably leads to lower visibility, especially during the exit portion of the dive. As listed below, low visibility can drastically slow the diver's exit, and compounded with small restrictions, can create a scenario where the gas planning rule of thirds would not be sufficient. In these cases, the minimum gas rule should be organized on fourths (one fourth of the gas supply is used for the inward portion of the dive, one forth is used for the exit and one half of the gas supply carried is held in reserve for emergencies). This technique has saved many divers who were stuck in low visibility caves.

Due to the increased task loading associated with switching second stage regulators, the diver must remember that both cylinder gauges must be monitored more frequently than if the standard cave diving configuration (i.e. doubles) was being used.

There are additional instances specific to side mount diving that warrant a more conservative approach to gas management, including:

1. Loss of visibility – The loss of visibility due to silting or primary light failure will drastically slow a

Trapped in a sump on the wrong side of a broken line, in zero visibility with minimal gas supplies, Wes Skiles once noted to his diving buddies, "the only people who can save us are already in the cave right now!" Patience and methodical thinking allowed the team to rescue themselves.

If you choose to solo dive or explore at the edge of the envelope, the risks are higher and chances for rescue become negligible. Self sufficiency and control are paramount.

diver's exit from a small, restricted cave. The ability to efficiently move through restrictions by following the guideline through physical contact without visual reference is slow and time consuming. Additional gas reserves should be considered when the chances of exiting a restricted cave are compounded by low visibility.

2. Gas sharing – Side mount cave diving demands a self sufficient mentality. Team members are available to assist each other with restrictions and line entanglements but gas sharing in small spaces could easily lead to a double fatality. A long hose for gas sharing is not necessarily used in side mount cave diving. There should never be a situation that requires air sharing, if the divers adhere to the rule of thirds, or fourths if appropriate, and a long hose may create an entanglement hazard for divers choosing to access small restrictions. The very nature of side mount caves makes air sharing an almost impossible feat.

3. Snags and restrictions – Restrictions force side mount cave divers into single file, in places that snag equipment. A Hollywood producer once noted that at one moment your dive buddy is an asset to the team and in the next moment, he is the "cork in the bottle that contains your life." For this reason, careful gas planning must include the potential delays caused by tight restrictions. Teams should plan on the self-sufficiency of each diver.

Visibility

Side mount divers will probably spend a greater portion of their dive in low to zero visibility than their back mount counterparts, especially if the cave they are diving is considered "side mount" for its entire length. In some of these side mount caves, proper finning techniques are futile. Visibility can be reduced to nothing as a result of the divers' bubbles, or in some cases, as the result of the pressure wave created when the diver moves through the water. Side mount divers must be prepared to deal with

ZERO VISIBILITY
TOUCH CONTACT
SIGNALS:

ONE SQUEEZE – HOLD
PUSH – MOVE FORWARD
PULL – MOVE BACKWARD

Tucking the thumb between the fingers is a tactile sign for "I'm stuck." If you are snagged in a restriction with no visibility, let your buddy feel your hand while you make this signal.

Side mount exploration may require advanced logistics and significant team preparation. Careful consideration of a "team" versus "lean solo" approach is critical.

emergency situations (for themselves or their partners) in low to zero visibility and realize that much, or all, of their exit from these small caves may have to be done by feel. The diver may or may not be able see their gas contents gauges for long periods of time, adding a sense of urgency to moving through a narrow or muddy section of cave. Divers should concentrate on slowing their breathing rates as soon as a tight, low visibility situation presents itself. Touch contact drills should be well rehearsed and careful consideration should be given to appropriate team size for particular cave conditions.

Guideline Use

A greater need for visual or physical contact with the guideline is another cause of stress. Most cave divers stay at least an arm's length from the guideline during their dive to prevent entanglements. In a small side mount passage, the diver may have no choice but to lie on, go under, or move the guideline in order to push through. In this scenario, the diver must pay more attention to line placement (i.e. line traps & entanglements) than in larger passages.

Negotiating Restrictions

When it comes to passage size or restrictions, how small is small? Most cave diving manuals describe a minor restriction as a place where two divers cannot swim side by side. A major restriction is considered to be a section of cave that causes a diver with back mounted cylinders to come into contact with the cave. Side mount divers would consider that a giant borehole passage. It's all relative to the experience of the diver(s). Each diver must decide whether attempting a restricted area is within his or her acceptable level of risk. This level of acceptable risk will vary for each diver and may be different for individuals on different dive plans and objectives.

Physical Orientation

Many times, side mount divers will encounter large breakdown areas where boulders jam a passage. In attempting to pass through these boulder chokes, the divers may become inverted. As Murphy's Law would have it, this is usually the moment when the diver floods their mask, regulator or becomes entangled in the guideline. The side mount diver should be comfortable being upside down (either horizontally or vertically) with a flooded mask or regulator. This skill can be practiced in shallow, open water so that the diver can become accustomed to the breathing resistance that occurs while in an inverted position. Divers should also keep in mind that the orientation required to pass a restriction on the inward portion of the dive will require a completely different approach upon exit. Stopping and examining the restriction after it has been passed may mentally prepare the diver for the exit ahead of time.

Getting Stuck

One of the first questions asked of cave divers is, "What do you do if you get stuck?" The same question is even more frequently asked of side mounters. The answer may be different for each person, though there are some important common insights:

1. DON'T PANIC

As in all diving activities, the ability to maintain a level head is critical. When a diver is unable to move in the direction they want to move, slowly, methodically moving the body, equipment or both will generally release snags. Slowing the breathing rate and

Kenny Broad rappels into a cave in a remote region of Abaco while being supported by the authors. Initial exploration is often conducted with very small tanks, before committing to a more complicated plan.

thinking each step of the process through will significantly minimize problems.

2. KNOW YOUR EQUIPMENT

Knowing every inch of your side mount rig, and being able to access every part by feel alone, will greatly reduce the amount of time spent undoing snags or being wedged into a particular place. The diver should be able to visualize every part of the rig and be able to find it, move it, and/or remove it. This can only come with time and repetitive practice. Some divers prefer to set up their configurations so that if they become wedged, they can unbuckle the entire system and swim out of it. This should be done only as an absolute last resort. Remember that becoming separated from your gas supply and ballast is a real threat in this situation.

An effective way to memorize your system is through simple visualization. Don the harness system, close your eyes and find every movable and removable piece of hardware. Repetitively remove and replace each item. Cylinder manipulation will be much easier to practice in the water, but the rest of the system can be rehearsed in street clothes on the surface. Touch recognition of all equipment is essential for efficient side mount technique.

3. ASK FOR HELP

If you have a buddy, ask for help. They may be able to see the point that is catching your gear. In poor visibility, use tactile signals to communicate.

4. WAIT AND ASSIST

If you just had difficulties in a restriction, chances are that your buddy will too. After you pass the restriction, the visibility will be lowered. You may need to help guide your buddy through the hazards that you just figured out.

Rich Courtney assists Matt Hubner with the butt-mounting of his primary light. In the event that a diver gets stuck, they will need to be able to remove their light underwater.

Mixed Teams Concept

As discussed, many side mount divers consider their activity a solo activity with little or no chance of efficiently providing gas during emergencies. There are several instances where they may be required to configure for an air sharing situation:

- Side mount cave diving instructors who must provide air sharing capabilities for students in training.
- Side mount divers who dive in mixed teams with back mount divers or CCR divers who must provide air sharing capabilities in order to fulfill team requirements for either of these configurations.
- Side mount teams where each team member feels more comfortable having another source of air during the dive (triple redundancy).

See Chapter Six for a detailed discussion on gas sharing techniques.

Dan Lins uses gaitors to reduce air trapping in his dry suit feet. This can be critical for divers who may need to invert in restricted passages.

Independent Diver Philosophy

Of all the equipment necessary for the side mount diver, one of the most important pieces is the diver's mindset. Even though side mount dives can be conducted in teams, the diver must consider himself to be alone in the cave with regard to rescue and gas supply.

Side mount caves are not conducive to rescue by another diver and thus 90% of the time the side mount diver's sole source of gas/rescue is him or herself. The side mount diver must feel comfortable being in confined spaces and alone for long periods of time. All problems must be solved underwater, in the cave, and usually on your own.

An adjustable "belly strap" (left diver) can be used to minimize the wing profile. Prior to a restriction, air may be dumped and the wing corners snugged down.

Side mount (in side mount caves) is considered a solo activity by most cave divers. The diver can move more efficiently into the side mount cave, and more importantly, can exit the cave faster alone than with a team of divers. Visibility is only reduced by a single diver rather than a team of divers, and there is no risk of being trapped behind a stuck diver in a zero-visibility restriction. Many feel these advantages outweigh the benefits of relying on a team member for rescue.

Even when you dive with a buddy, a side mount diver will need to remain independent. Restrictions may require you to be self sufficient if you become snagged. It is for this reason that diving in smaller caves is considered an advanced activity.

Above all, the side mount diver should have the experience and confidence that they will be able to maintain control, breathing rate and composure within confined, low visibility passages.

Diver Propulsion Vehicles

Small caves are not suitable for scootering, but side mount cave divers may find that DPVs reduce transit times to remote corners of the system. Tow-behind models are preferred over ride-on scooters because of their low profile. Careful adjustment of trim weights and the tow strap are essential for permitting comfortable travel and one-handed operation of the scooter.

Frequent regulator swaps require that the diver be proficient in one-handed regulator switches. Second stages need to be placed high on the chest to prevent free-flowing from the prop wash. Advanced side mount divers who are using stage bottles should sling them on top of primary tanks or top-clip them to the hip after use to maximize streamlining.

Careful organization and marking of second stages and SPGs will help the diver keep track of tank pressures. A disorganized kit may cause confusion over SPGs and second stages that results in using too much gas from one or another cylinder.

Driving a DPV in a cave is a specialized activity that requires additional training with an instructor who has experience side mounting and piloting scooters. Practice and conservative gas planning are essential. Experience must be gained in open water and large spaces before anything small is attempted, otherwise unnecessary damage to the cave environment may result.

Side mount configuration can be a comfortable configuration for cave divers whether they intend to dive in small passages or not. Popular all over the world, it can be the most convenient and adaptable configuration for travel.

ADVANCED SIDE MOUNT DIVING

CHAPTER

9

Advanced Side Mount Diver

Overview

The Advanced Side Mount Diver course presents techniques that are commonly used for longer penetrations and for cave exploration. This course exposes the qualified, experienced side mount cave diver to techniques and configurations that will allow them to safely and efficiently make full use of the side mount configuration, including single and double cylinder removals for accessing very small restrictions and passages. Technical dive planning is reviewed and enhanced including considerations for more complex gas management, increased task loading and challenging emergency scenarios.

Course lectures and in-water skills include:
- Stage diving
- Extended penetrations
- Single and double cylinder removals at major restrictions
- Overview using a specially-rigged cylinder for no-mount diving
- Mixed teams concepts – back mount and side mount teams/gas sharing emergencies
- Independent diving philosophy

Prerequisites

It is highly recommended that divers entering this level of training have completed a minimum of 50 cave dives after completion of their Full Cave Course and Side Mount Diver Course as well as have a Nitrox certification and be at least 18 years of age.

Stage Diving

The need for refined gas planning is required when including stage cylinders in a dive plan. The diver should know their Surface Air Consumption Rate (SAC Rate) and should be able to extrapolate gas needs based on distance, time and depth of the planned dive. It is highly recommended that a safety factor be included in the gas plan with respect to actual volume of gas required for the dive.

The use of stage cylinders for extending time or penetration is accomplished in much the same way as back mount. The only real changes are in configuration.

One of the key advantages for side mount configuration is the ability to remove and replace cylinders easily. The same applies for stage cylinders in this configuration.

The basic principle is to configure the additional stage cylinders in a way that allows for ease of removal and replacement as needed during the dive. A standard aluminum 80 cft (11 liter) cylinder is currently considered the optimum stage cylinder due to the amount of gas they contain versus size and weight with regard to trim and streamlining.

In stage diving, the cylinder is added either on top of or beneath the side mounted cylinder through the use of various attachment points (usually two). Instructors may refer to these different techniques as "over-slung" and "under-slung." Bolt snaps or boat clips (also referred to as suicide clips) are placed on the neck of the cylinder, around the valve and

Advanced side mount divers may need additional training in other aspects of exploration, such as Single Rope Technique (SRT), orienteering and safe caving. Exploration may involve remote operations that require significant logistics, emergency planning and extended risk.

A diver dons over-slung stage cylinders (above).

around the body, using a stainless steel hose clamp and bungee or cam-band, clip and bungee.

The lengths of these attachment points will vary greatly based on a diver's proportions. The use of a sturdy bungee cord for attachment will allow for ease of use when removing/replacing the cylinder and will help to keep the cylinder tucked in to the diver's side while swimming. Strong, double-braided nylon line may also be used for these attachment points, if the "stretch factor" is not needed to accommodate fit. The use of metal-to-metal attachment points is highly discouraged since these points cannot be cut away in the event of a serious entanglement or entrapment in a restriction.

As with back mount stage diving, the stages are breathed prior to using the primary, side mounted cylinders. Each stage is breathed down to 1/3 of its starting pressure (or less to be conservative), and then dropped. The stage(s) are retrieved during exit and the cylinder is used for another third during egress. The entire sequence can and should be done while slowly swimming (or scootering) in the appropriate direction of travel. Anticipation of a change in buoyancy after the drop/pickup will make this task more efficient and conserve both energy and gas.

The diver should be aware of the increase in breathing rate while trying to swim or scooter with multiple stage cylinders. Stage diving is more efficient while riding DPVs, but the cave configuration may or may not allow for the use of these devices.

At some point, stage diving becomes inefficient because of the number of cylinders that must be carried. Eventually set up dives are required in order to cache stage cylinders further into the cave for use in future penetrations.

The team concept works well when setting up stage caches and allows one or two divers to extend penetration with the help of other divers. In this type of stage diving, there are a minimum of three dives made: the setup dive where cylinders are dropped for the penetration team, the penetration dive, and the cleanup dive, where all cached cylinders are collected and returned to the surface.

Efficient Use of Stages

DROPPING THE STAGE CYLINDER

While continuing to swim through the cave the diver should:

- Once 1/3 or less of gas supply in stage is used, switch to alternate stage or side mounted cylinders.
- Stow away second stage on cylinder properly.
- Switch gas percentage on computer as required.
- Remove stage cylinder.
- Secure gas supply valve on stage cylinder and check for leaks.
- Find appropriate place to clip off stage bottle on guideline. This area should be away from deep mud, fragile formations, directly on the guideline and easily seen from a distance if possible. Stage cylinders should only be dropped in locations where damage will not occur to the cave or the cylinder. Upon reaching thirds or less, a diver will stop breathing from a cylinder, but may need to swim it for several more minutes until a safe drop zone can be identified.
- Anticipate change in buoyancy when stage is dropped.

The bottom clip is removed first. After removing the top clip, the diver stows their gear while swimming to the safe drop zone.

95

• Secure the stage cylinder to the guideline with a double wrap on one of the cylinder connections.
• Secure the second stage within easy reach on the cylinder or the guideline in case there is an emergency during the return trip.
• Double check that the gas supply is shut off.

When a team of divers is dropping stage bottles, they should consider spacing the cylinders apart so that they may be retrieved in order by the team without creating an unnecessary backlog. When cylinders are separated by a body length or more, divers may simultaneously pick up their cylinders and continue to exit more efficiently.

Stage drops and recoveries should be done while swimming and neutrally buoyant. A diver should only need to pause briefly to secure the cylinder to the line.

Lower stage clip secured with solid rubber bungee.

RECOVERING THE STAGE CYLINDER

Upon return to the stage cylinder, the diver should:
• Anticipate change in buoyancy when the stage cylinder is lifted.
• While neutrally buoyant, remove the stage from the line and open the cylinder valve.
• Continue swimming while checking pressure in the cylinder and ensuring there is no mud, rocks or critters in the mouthpiece of the second stage.
• Appropriately mount the cylinder to the harness.
• Switch breathing to the new stage cylinder.
• Switch gas percentage on computer as required.

Stage bottles should be recognizable by feel. Divers must be able to find their own cylinder in zero visibility, determine the gas content of the cylinder and don it while maintaining contact with the guideline. Unique regulators, different clips and tactile devices such as zip ties can help to differentiate bottles by feel. Divers should practice donning bottles with eyes closed to enhance memory retention for unique tactile devices.

Boat snaps rarely jam in sand and snap quickly with one hand.

Small Passages

Often times, the passage configuration of the cave will not be wide enough to allow for the stage cylinder to be worn on the diver's sides. In this case, the cylinder or cylinders are removed and hand held by the valve, with the bottom of the cylinder pointing into the cave. Once the passage becomes large enough to sling the stage cylinder once again, it is replaced on the diver's side in the appropriate position.

In the case of a very small passage, where even the side mounted cylinders must also be removed, the stages are "ferried" one at a time through the restriction in order to get the appropriate gas supply on the far side. This may even require that one stage cylinder be sacrificed and breathed during the ferrying process and left at the restriction.

Extended Penetrations

With the addition of stage cylinders, the diver is exposed to increased environmental and physical factors over diving with only two cylinders. These additional risks include:

INCREASED BOTTOM TIMES
- Increased penetrations and/or distance from the surface.
- Increased potential for thermal issues.
- Increased decompression obligation requiring additional gas and exposure protection.
- Increased number of small or long restrictions in the course of the dive.
- Increased chance of equipment malfunction. The more gear that is put into the water, the greater the chance that something will eventually fail.
- Increased depth in some systems requiring multiple stages of varying gas mixtures.

Extended penetrations can psychologically affect the diver. The diver can experience time/distance stress that can increase breathing rate and gas use. Exhaustion is not only a physical condition. Mental stress, task loading and distance pressure add to overall fatigue.

SINGLE AND DOUBLE CYLINDER REMOVALS FOR RESTRICTIONS
While the side mount configuration itself allows the diver to move through small areas, the design of today's side mount harnesses also allows us to easily remove one or both cylinders to access even smaller restrictions.

In a Nutshell

DROPPING A STAGE:
1. Use 1/3 or less.
2. Switch to new cylinder.
3. Stow gear.
4. Switch computer.
5. Remove stage cylinder.
6. Check for leaks.
7. Find safe drop zone.
8. Anticipate buoyancy.
9. Check gas is shut off.
10. Clip to line.

RECOVERING A STAGE:
1. Anticipate buoyancy change.
2. Unclip from line.
3. Turn on gas.
4. Keep swimming.
5. Look for leaks.
6. Replace cylinder on body when safe to do so, and cave won't be damaged.
7. Stow gear.
8. Switch to new cylinder.
9. Switch computer.
10. Breathe new cylinder on exit.

There are two key hazards that must be considered when conducting cylinder removals:

• Separation from ballast - As soon as a diver removes a cylinder, he or she must be prepared for loss of ballast. This can be catastrophic if the cylinders are removed in a large room or over a fissure prior to a restriction.

• Separation from gas supply - In the same scenario as above, the diver stands to lose not only their ballast, but their entire gas supply if the cylinder is not tethered in a secure manner.

In a single cylinder removal, unclip the lower attachment and outstretch your arm to extend the cylinder forward. Leave the upper attachment in place if possible. Tuck your chin down to reduce your profile and delicately pass through the restriction.

Before passing any narrow restriction, the diver should assess the following:

• Gas available for passing the restriction and further penetration.
• Size of the restriction.
• Team gas supplies.
• Back referencing.

Once on the far side of the restriction, the diver should assess the return route for "one-way" snags to ensure that he/she will be able to pass the restriction without delay once the dive has been called and guarantee that both gas supply and visibility will be sufficient. The return trip will be slowed significantly when multiple restrictions are negotiated by a team of side mount divers. Gas planning should take into consideration a delayed return to the exit.

In some cases, tanks will be passed through a restriction from one diver to another. Tanks should never be set down on the floor of the cave without being first clipped to the guideline. A cylinder, or any other piece of equipment, can be easily lost in breakdown or fissure cracks. It can also be "lost" in silty conditions. All tanks should be identifiable by feel.

Helmet-mounted lights may prove to be beneficial in restrictions when the diver's hands are busy with cylinder removals and guideline management.

No-Mount Diving

At some point, the side mount diver will encounter a restriction too small to pass with any cylinders attached to the harness. In this case a "no-mount" cylinder can be used in order to a pass body-sized restriction. The no-mount cylinder can be any size

Whenever you pass through a restriction, it is important to assess whether the return trip will present more challenges. Stay conservative and don't forget to empty your wing to get small.

Brian Kakuk prepares for a no-mount squeeze. The cylinder on the left, with two regulators and an H-valve will be retained for breathing. Other cylinders are fed through afterward by his partner.

SCUBA cylinder, but is rigged with a single, dual-outlet valve (also known as an H-valve, Y-valve or Modular valve). This cylinder can be rigged as one of the side mount cylinders or as a stage to be used only when the small restriction is encountered.

The no-mount cylinder will have two separate regulators, each with its own first and second stages. Only one of these regulators is required to have a high pressure gauge for monitoring its gas contents. The backup second stage is secured in an easy to reach place at the top of the cylinder, while the primary second stage is secured to the diver's neck by a bungee cord necklace. A small buoyancy wing can be wrapped around larger or heavier no-mount cylinders to make the entire system neutral.

The most important piece of equipment needed on the no-mount cylinder is a strong tether made of either 1/2 inch bungee cord or nylon line. The cylinder tether is secured around the cylinder valve and then to the diver. The length of the tether must be shorter than the length of the primary second stage hose, but still allow the cylinder to be pushed ahead of the diver efficiently.

Gas planning for no-mount diving must be extremely conservative. Maximum penetration on a no-mount cylinder should be no more than quarters rather than thirds (i.e. one quarter gas used in, one quarter gas used out, and the remainder used for reserve).

In addition to the tethered attachment points, the no-mount cylinder should also be rigged for either

mounting as a stage or as one of the side mounted cylinders. If it is used as one of the side mounts, the cylinder size should match the same cylinder used on the opposite side. In other words, if the diver's no-mount cylinder is a steel 85, then the opposite side mount cylinder should also be a steel 85 for balance.

Valve and cylinder maintenance on the no-mount cylinder is paramount. Burst discs should be changed often and valve-to-cylinder o-rings should be changed at least every 6 months. The diver should remember that he/she is carrying a very finite amount of gas and separation from or loss of this gas will be fatal.

No-mount restrictions are not generally traversed by teams. In cases where a team dives together, only one diver goes through the restricted area unless prior knowledge indicates that turning around is possible. Specialized hand and light signals should be organized before the dive so the waiting buddy knows when assistance is required. All emergency scenarios should be discussed and rehearsed prior to diving so that each diver knows their roles and responsibilities and is willing to take on the additional risk of this type of diving.

Both the back mount and side mount divers carry long hoses for air sharing. It is critical that the side mount diver balance air use to ensure for adequate reserves in the case of an emergency.

SUMP DIVING

CHAPTER 10

Sump Diving Background

Sump diving, which combines remote dry caving with cave diving, is the most advanced form of side mount cave diving. The genesis of cave diving in many countries was often inspired by spelunkers who reached a terminal room and wondered what lay beneath the surface of the water. Some of the first instances of sump diving were free-swims under rock ceilings to search for more dry passage beyond. Due to their heavy weight and fragile manifolds, back mounted doubles were deemed unsuitable for sump diving with small side mount cylinders being preferred.

A diver passing through Sump Two at France's La Font du Truffe using Martyn Farr's very streamlined *Explorer 1* harness with a drysuit as buoyancy. Photo: Courtesy of Martyn Farr

One of the earliest recorded sump dives was attempted by an Englishman, John Bray. He was determined to "dive under a rock and rise in the cavern beyond." Unfortunately he struck his head on the ceiling underwater and fell motionless to the floor of the cave. Luckily, his buddies were able to recover him, but not without difficulty. In years to follow, attempts to pass the sump became more determined. At one point, the sump was artificially drained, but explorers realized there needed to be a better way to traverse water hazards and gain a foothold on the other side.

In 1934, Jack Sheppard and Graham Balcombe engineered a home-made respirator from a women's bicycle frame and other spare parts around their garage. They attempted to pass a sump in Swildon's Hole in the Mendip Hills of England. Though unsuccessful on that day, they ignited a fire of interest among fellow cavers, that water filled sumps might be passable. Soon after, they made a successful voyage through sumps in Wookey Hole. Using pipe, a homemade football pump, lights and a telephone, they brought high technology to speleologists. These

men, with other members of the British Cave Diving Group (CDG), used rebreathers to pass water filled sumps in the 1940s. It was only logical that side mount technique would soon follow as a more efficient means to transport tanks through a cave.

It is often necessary to travel through significant expanses of dry cave before reaching the point where diving technology must be used. Cavers are notorious for doing anything they can to avoid the risk and gear associated with diving. Many would rather climb than swim. Yet, as more divers get involved in sump exploration, it seems the reverse is true - a cave diver would almost always prefer swimming over rigging and climbing.

Brian Williams and Matt Vinzant assessing the muddy water at the Logsdon River Sump in Roppel Cave, Kentucky - part of the largest system in the world, Mammoth Cave.

Risks of Sump Diving

Regardless of the motivation for sump diving, there are many specific risks that must be considered. Sump diving is the most dangerous type of cave diving.

Remote Access

Many sumps are located at great distances from the cave opening. In addition to the risk of *diving* in remote locations, the dry caving activity itself can be very dangerous. A relatively minor injury can be life

ARE YOU PREPARED?

How to be a sump diver:
1. Become a spelunker.
2. Get SRT training.
3. Find a mentor.
4. Volunteer as a sherpa.
5. Perfect side mount skills.
6. Practice with new gear.
7. Be excellent with reels.
8. Practice restrictions.
9. Get fit for caving.
10. Get mentally fit.

JOIN AN ORGANIZATION:

The following are a few active organizations and sump diving projects:
1. The National Speleological Society: www.caves.org
2. The Cave Diving Group: www.CaveDivingGroup.co.uk
3. The Cave Divers Association of Australia: www.cavedivers.com.au
4. The United States Deep Caving Team Inc.: www.usdct.org
5. Cave Conservancy of Hawaii: www.hawaiicaves.org
6. Ukrainian Youth Caver Exchange: www.uaycef.org
7. Texas Speleological Association: www.cavetexas.org

threatening when you are a long distance from the surface. A sprained ankle on the far side of a sump can result in shock, hypothermia and death.

When an entire team chooses to commit to diving a sump and exploring beyond, the chances for rescue are minimized. Oftentimes, the best people to launch a rescue are already cold, exhausted and in the cave.

Vertical work

Climbing skills and equipment may be required. Divers may have to rappel, climb and rig dangerous pitches. Single Rope Technique (SRT) is often needed. Gear may need to be lowered or raised over hazards and can be damaged prior to arrival at the sump. Teamwork is essential to safety.

Variable Conditions

Many dry caves are known to flood in various weather scenarios. A perfect setup location may submerge underwater in a matter of hours or minutes. A clean rappel can turn into a raging waterfall. Personnel can be trapped below water hazards. Local experience is critical.

Fatigue and Hypothermia

Physical and mental stresses including exhaustion and cold take a toll on cavers, who may be working on missions that span 12 or more hours of continuous effort. There may be no place to rest comfortably or warm up if somebody gets excessively chilled.

Limited Resources

Sump diving is always a give and take exercise. It is often impossible to get the gear you want back to a sump, so careful risk assessment makes divers consider every item for its usefulness. British cavers often sacrifice fins, reasoning that their caving boots are more useful on the other side. With limited visibility, it may be more prudent to make a quick stomp through a short sump than to carry fins for a needless swim. Other divers sacrifice bright primary lights since lighter backups are all that may be needed in small passages. Carrying a six-hour primary light may be pointless if you only need to penetrate a 500-foot sump. Any gear sacrifice may increase risk exposure.

Planning a Sump Dive

Determine a Purpose

Given the complexity of sump exploration, a simple purpose should be established to help organize the framework for a particular dive. For exam-

ple, the first time an explorer reaches a sump, they may plan to simply free dive with a mask and light to make an assessment of whether a dive has any merit. Goals should be clear and manageable, and all participants should be reminded that, whether they are wet or dry, they have the ability and duty to "call the dive" at any time, including prior to reaching the water.

Assessment of the Cave

As with any submerged cave, sumps have their own unique character and features. A review of these features is critical to the planning process. The review should include discussion of the following topics.

- Geography: distance to sump
- Restrictions: type of passages prior to reaching sump (walk, crawl, restrictions, drops)

Sump diving entails significant risk and effort just getting yourself and your gear to the site.

- Cave type: breakdown, streams, loose material, drops, fragile features (such as speleothems)
- Dive entry: muddy, steep, how to get in and out of water, risks to visibility
- Navigation: what aids are needed to find the ultimate destination?
- Conditions: cave air temperature, dry or wet prior to sump? Are walls hard or jagged?
- Other items in cave: fixed lines, navigation aids, bones, fossils, garbage dumps
- Anticipated diving conditions: current, visibility, cave substrate, previously laid line hazards, speleothems, halocline, water temperature
- Activities to be conducted on the far side of the sump
- Chance of elevated carbon dioxide (bad air) or other gaseous hazards
- Cave diving conditions: anything known about depth, distance, visibility or egress on the far side of the sump
- Additional gear: silt screws, SRT gear, food, water, spare lights, etc.

Assemble a Team

Several types of personnel are required to execute a successful sump dive. The largest contingent may be support personnel who act as sherpas that carry gear to the water. It may take several trips over several days to transport all the gear to the water's edge. Loads may need to be divided into small packages to be manageable. Surface-based personnel may be employed for organization, safety and emergencies.

The dive team is usually the smallest portion of the group, although rotating teams are often employed. On one particular day you may be a gear sherpa; the following day you may be a dive team leader; the next day you may have a topside role to rest and stand-by for emergencies.

All team members need to be well trained in their particular role, yet flexibility and versatility within the team is paramount.

Equipment Planning

Any gear that is carried to a sump will be subjected to impact, shock, submersion, abrasion and lots of mud. Sump diving gear needs to be of the highest quality to survive these impacts. It must be packed well in small loads. Anything that becomes unmanageable is usually subjected to even more damage by a tired sherpa.

TANKS

Plan to use the smallest tanks possible to get the job done safely. Carefully consider whether aluminum or steel tanks will be the best choice. Many people select aluminum because they are lighter. Steel tanks might be unmanageable to carry to the sump. If weight is needed for buoyancy, it can be left in the cave permanently and carried in separate loads.

Manifolds are completely unsuitable for sump diving because of the likelihood of damage in transport. Tank valves must be protected by either a valve plug or regulator. This way, if the sherpa accidentally knocks the valve into the "on" position, leakage is less likely. If you use valve plugs, be sure they are the type that can be vented without tools, so that you can get them out easily. Otherwise, bring a large wrench.

Tanks are rarely carried without protection. Most divers choose to place tanks in a hauling bag that is rigged with many different types of straps. The sherpa may want to carry the bag over their shoulder when walking, but may have to tether the tank to their ankle to pull through a long crawl. The tank bag may need to be lowered on rope or dragged on the ground. Wrapping the tank (and regulator if it is installed) in a foam sleeping pad before putting it in the bag offers the best protection, as well as flotation, in stream-filled passages.

Brian Williams, Matt Vinzant and Mark Wenner carefully pack small loads for transport through Roppel Cave. Their bags have multiple rigging straps and are smooth-skinned and watertight, to prevent mud from weighing down the pack and contaminating equipment.

Canadian caver Scott Bauer slides down a clay slope leading to a sump. Even muddy areas can be dangerous, since ascending might be impossible without a hand-line.

HARNESS

It is recommended to use a side mount harness that can be worn through the cave to get to the sump. Integrated canyoneering harnesses such as the newest Armadillo rig are favorable. Some other harnesses may be worn with a seat harness for rappelling. In many cases, the simplest webbed harness will be all that is needed in the sump.

BUOYANCY

Many sump divers do not use wings for buoyancy. These divers reason that sumps are either short and permit crawling, or they choose to use their dry suit for buoyancy. Since small tanks are the norm in sump diving, negative buoyancy is rarely an issue. Positive buoyancy is more often the problem to overcome.

REGULATORS

Yoke-style connections are not suitable for sump diving because they may be dislodged in transit. Yoke knobs are very vulnerable to damage. If the regulator is not installed on the tank, it should be carried in a padded bag. The inlet should be covered with a threaded, sealed cap to protect from mud and dirt, and to secure and protect the DIN o-ring.

LIGHTS

Primary canister lights are generally not used, except for long sumps. Smaller lights may be all that is needed for a short or low visibility sump. Lights that are only burnable underwater are considered an unnecessary weight burden. Every light needs to double as a surface light.

LED bulbs are more robust than HID lights. In a nutshell, lights must be reliable and durable. Many sump divers wear their lights on their helmet, although a hand-held light sometimes penetrates turbid water more effectively. Most cavers carry a minimum of five light sources, since lights are used for long durations in the dry part of the cave too. Rather than carrying and protecting spare batteries, cavers usually carry spare lights instead. As with all waste, dead batteries must be transported out of the cave, so they might as well be encased in a small protected flashlight.

THERMAL PROTECTION

Wet suits are sometimes worn in the cave, just to get to the site. However, anything thicker than a 2-3 mm suit may prove to be restrictive to movement and breathing. Wearing a soggy wetsuit for many hours makes it difficult to re-warm after submersion. Consideration should be given to the additional safety of using a dry suit.

The cons of dry suits are: they can get damaged in transit, they are too warm for dry caving and they must be carried in a separate water-tight bag. The pro is that they may be used for dry storage for things that are taken through the sump. Food and dry clothing may be carried inside a dry suit for caving on the other side.

Whether you wear a wet suit or caving coveralls to get to the sump, you will need knee and elbow protection for many caves. If you plan to take these through the sump, ensure that they are of a type that minimizes positive buoyancy.

Dry suit repair kits or replacement Zip-seals may be carried to manage seal failures at the dive site.

FOOTWEAR

Some drysuits have sock-type feet that permit use of Rock Boots or Caving Boots. These are beneficial to minimize loads. Carrying additional wet suit boots is a waste of precious resources, since they are rarely rugged enough to double as caving boots for the dry work.

Sturdy footwear is essential for transit to the sump.

A sturdy, large reel will be needed to carry line. Small, plexiglass or lightweight plastic models are unlikely to survive the rigors of transport.

111

FINS

Fins may or may not be necessary for the type of sump you are anticipating. If you can manage without them, it alleviates carrying a large item. When diving with alternating groups, fins and most other equipment can be shared.

MASK

It goes without saying that a mask is important. However, given that sumps rarely have visibility, you may decide to sacrifice a spare mask or carry one spare per team. The mask should be protected in a lightweight box or padding for travel purposes.

REELS

Common plexiglass or plastic reels are rarely durable enough to make it to a sump unharmed. As with all equipment, it will be dragged, dropped and dumped and must be able to withstand the rigors of cave hauling. Sometimes safety reels are not used if the explorer will be carrying the reel in their hand at all times while they run line in an easy, short sump. Instead, each diver carries a full-sized exploration reel. All line should be knotted at proper increments for exploration.

Homemade reels are very common in sump exploration. Sturdy reels made to accommodate thicker line are often used. Some sumps have tremendous flow - it was reported in one UK cave that galvanized chain had to be installed in the cave after 11mm line was shredded in the current. Cold water and high flow may dictate the need for a line that can withstand pulling to get through a high flow sump.

LINE MARKERS

Depending on the weight of line, traditional line markers may not fit. Other marking techniques may need to be developed if required. Some divers use clothes pins, while others make custom plastic arrows for heavy line.

COMPUTERS

Some divers use a simple bottom timer and watch while others prefer the audible alarms that come with proper diving computers. In a no visibility scenario, these devices can guide you through decompression based on audio beeps. Spares are also important since this is not just a planning tool, but also your critical data-carrying device for cave survey.

DATA COLLECTION TOOLS

Slates, notebooks and pencils are needed to collect survey data. These are traditionally stowed in a "man-purse" (described in Chapter Three) and clipped to a rear D-ring.

HELMET

A proper, certified climbing helmet is necessary for both dry and wet portions of the cave. Even minor head injuries can pose a huge risk for the whole team.

DIVING TOOLS

A small tool kit for a team of divers may save a project. These minimal items may also be used as ballast in positively buoyant packs. Before you carry lead weights into a cave, consider whether there is a more useful tool that can provide the necessary negative buoyancy. A wrench is more useful than a square block of lead and will weigh the same to the person carrying it. A trowel or small shovel may be a useful item. A pry bar is heavy and can weigh down a sump pack while providing other useful purposes.

EMERGENCY EQUIPMENT

First aid, safety blankets and other contingency gear should be managed and shared as a group.

SILT SCREWS

Some caves are bereft of good tie-offs. In these cases, PVC silt screws may be used to create a solid belay or tie off. Tent pegs may also serve the same purpose.

SUMP PACKS OR TUBES

If you plan to cave or camp on the other side of the sump, then a sump pack or solid tube will need to be carried to contain dry equipment for the other side. Camping is beyond the scope of this manual, but consideration for items such as food, water purification and a stove may be important whether you

A British sump or "tackle" bag that may be used for gear or small tanks. Note the narrow profile, slick durable material and numerous rigging options. Straps are rarely padded, since foam collects mud, which weighs down the pack. Courtesy: Martyn Farr

Beyond the travel through the cave, your gear may be subjected to even further hazards before you go diving. Protecting the gas inside the tanks by placing a valve plug in the DIN fitting will also protect threads from dirt and damage.

camp or not. Sump packs and tubes are buoyant. You may need significant weight to get them underwater. This should be rehearsed prior to beginning a project.

HAULING PACKS

All gear will need to be divided into light, manageable loads. Packs should be durable, abrasion resistant and in some cases waterproof. Packs need ample, secure hauling straps for lowering and dragging. They should not be made of a material that will absorb and carry mud. Muddy packs get saturated and heavy.

Plan the Dive

General aspects of dive planning remain the same in terms of organizing depth, time and contingency plans. Additional consideration must be given to the fact that significant physical effort may be needed to get back out of the cave. Decompression stress should be minimized. Depths and durations should be extremely conservative. Divers should conserve energy prior to the dive and beware of heavy workloads afterward. It may be more important to exit the cave and rest after a dive, than to start lugging heavy gear, taking an unnecessary risk of decompression illness.

Navigational Plan

Assemble all the tools for navigation that will be needed and review them as a team. These items include: cave map, survey markers, compasses and guidelines. Discuss other factors that may come into play, such as water flow and references. If a guide is used, make a plan for staying together with the guide, but continue personally referencing forward and back as you travel. In the event that you are separated from the guide or need to divide into smaller rescue groups, you must be able to navigate back to the surface without help.

Solo diving may be considered after careful analysis of all risks.

Risk Assessment

Anticipate the hazards that groups and individuals may experience in both dry caving and underwater environments. Since conditions can change within a cave over time, planning should include anticipating the worst possible conditions. Discuss breakdown piles, unstable slopes, changing weather conditions, flooding, getting lost, entanglement, decompression emergencies, effects of stress and potential injuries.

Stress Assessment

Identify likely sources of stress and discuss techniques for prevention and mitigation. There are many foreseeable situations that can cause stress to an individual, including darkness, silt-out, getting lost, cold, exhaustion, injury, distance-pressure (psychological stress caused from being a long distance from the surface) and gear failures.

Rehearsal

New techniques and equipment should never be undertaken the first time during exploration. Re-

Steve Omeroid rigs the first drop into Roppel Cave.

A group of eager cavers awaits instructions and loads while they assist sump divers in rigging a cave in Kentucky.

hearsal is imperative to reduce risk. Rehearsal can include the following scenarios for individuals and the team: communications, new gear, swimming with sump packs, using silt screws, buoyancy with additional gear inside drysuit, working without fins, negotiating restrictions, line laying technique, and survey and emergency procedures, such as using a litter to manage the rescue of an accident victim.

Solo Diving

Solo diving happens during sump exploration, whether intentional or accidental. Low visibility separates divers that swim together, but more often, divers choose to solo dive. If passages are small, then it may be safer to dive alone. Even though you won't have a redundant brain along for the dive, at least the stress of worrying about somebody else is relieved. There will be nobody blocking your exit, damaging tie-offs, causing silt or offering up a false sense of security. Whether you dive alone or with somebody else you must enter the water and dive self-sufficient. You should re-evaluate the dive altogether if you are not capable of self-rescue and buddy-rescue.

Arrival at the Sump

Once you arrive at the dive site, diving equipment will need to be unpacked, assembled and tested. Sometimes it is worth bringing a tarp through the cave to provide a clean work and dressing area. Sump packs should be organized for the through trip. Gear left behind should be carefully stowed above the high water line.

Support Personnel

Support personnel, often referred to as "sherpas," are critical to the success and safety of sump diving. It is often unreasonable to assume that you will be able to get all of your equipment to a sump without assistance. Risk assessment must include the dangers that support personnel face. Sherpas often feel pressured to perform any task they are given. They may put themselves at risk, feeling the obligation to make a successful mission. Once you arrive at the dive site, support personnel may stay on, have other duties, or return to the surface. If they are needed to "babysit," then consideration must be given to their comfort. After a lot of hard work, it is easy to get dangerously chilled.

Support personnel deserve your gratitude. Without their help, you'll never get in the water. Be sure to thank them while rewarding them with pictures and data.

Line Laying

Laying line in a sump may be very similar to laying line in restricted side mount passages. It may however, have another purpose. Sometimes hand lines are laid through sumps to allow others to pass through quickly without the need for fins. In this case, a heavy climbing rope is laid right through the middle of the passage. Sometimes the followers clip in to the line. In high flow, divers may use ascenders to grip the rope and pull through the current.

In some cases, line is also laid in the dry portion leading up to or between sumps. If the passage is likely to be flooded on this or subsequent trips, then laying a dry line will facilitate quick navigation.

Many sumps are subjected to seasonal high flows that tear away poorly laid line. Heavier gauge rope and very solid tie offs may be necessary if you hope to use that line in the future.

Sump diving is a widely varied sport. From simple traverses to harrowing descents through waterfalls and underground lakes, sump diving has many risks. It is impossible for this text to offer anything more than a cursory foundation. Sump diving should be undertaken cautiously, with local knowledge and under the guidance of a mentor. Apprenticing with a skilled local caver will help you gain knowledge, learn about risks and create a safe plan.

PROFILES

11

CHAPTER

Advice from the Experts

The use of current side mount systems has evolved from the hard work and innovation of not only the individuals listed previously, but also the hard work of manufacturers who have strived to bring these systems into the main stream as an alternative to classic back mount diving.

This chapter highlights equipment and divers who the authors feel have made significant contributions to the current popularity of side mount configuration. Each diver explains why they have chosen their current rig, any modifications they have made, and the pros and cons of their system.

Jakub Rehacek

Owner, Golem Gear

SIDE MOUNT HAMMERHEAD CCR

Q: What is the base of your system?

Golem Gear manufactures and sells the Armadillo Exploration side mount harness, as well as the Armadillo CCR side mount kit, which provides attachment points for carrying ultimately streamlined bailout bottles for any rebreather.

The Armadillo Exploration side mount harness is also a base platform for the Hammerhead CCR side mount configuration.

Golem Gear worked closely with Brett Hemphill and Curt Bowen on design and development of the Armadillo Exploration side mount harness. The A2 model has a number of improvements. The extremely strong and abrasion/puncture resistant materials are used for both the inner bladder and the wing cover. The interchangeable dump valve/ inflation hose were moved to the left side. Additional attachment points were added after divers' feedback.

Q: Please give a brief history on the evolution of this kit.

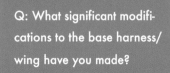

Armadillo CCR was designed in 2004 as an add-on kit for rebreathers to eliminate the "dangling bailout bottle" syndrome so prevalent in early rebreather diving. Today, it is by far the most popular CCR accessory used by rebreather divers worldwide.

The Hammerhead CCR side mount configuration was developed in 2009 to serve the needs of explorer CCR divers. This configuration was made to support Bill Gambrill's O_2 bottle cage. It uses the Armadillo Exploration side mount harness as an attachment platform and Hammerhead Hobo CCR with back mounted counter lungs for streamlined side mount CCR setup.

No modifications to the base harness are needed, since the Armadillo is purpose designed for side mount diving. It is the most streamlined and line-trap-free commercially available side mount system. The single piece construction was developed from the most rugged materials for expedition-type exploration in remote areas.

Q: What significant modifications to the base harness/ wing have you made?

In the Hammerhead CCR side mount configuration we have attached the back mounted counterlungs (BMCLs) to the Armadillo Exploration harnesses. Special 90-degree T-pieces facilitate hose routing to the side mounted Hammerhead Hobo CCR. This configuration provides for clear chest while still keeping the back of the Armadillo smooth and streamlined.

Q: What do you feel is the strongest advantage of your kit in side mount caves?

The streamlined and line-trap-free side mount system and the single piece construction developed from the most rugged materials available. There are a multitude of attachment points for survey equipment and photo/video gear. It can be (and has been) used with climbing harnesses to rappel into cenotes and easily attach bottles while floating.

The Hammerhead CCR side mount configuration is the ideal tool for diving side mount caves with CCR. The CCR can be unclipped at the hip to be pushed through restrictions in the same manner as any side mounted bottle.

Q: What do you feel is the strongest advantage of your kit in back mount caves?

The Armadillo Exploration side mount harness can be used in back mount caves and the diver will reap all the benefits mentioned above. The Armadillo can also be configured with a third bottle (or small doubles) attached to the center of the harness on the diver's back.

The Armadillo CCR kit can (and should) be used with any back mount configuration to streamline the stage bottles.

The Hammerhead CCR side mount configuration is the ideal tool for diving back mount caves, especially those with high flow. The low profile streamlined configuration of side mounted CCR reduces drag substantially.

The Armadillo Exploration side mount harness can be used in open water. It can be configured with a bottle attached to the center of the harness on the diver's back the same way as any single tank BC, only much more streamlined. The Armadillo Exploration side mount harness should be in every dive bag as a part of a "save a dive" kit when a primary harness or rebreather fails.

Q: Is this suitable for open water diving?

The Armadillo CCR kit can be used with any back mount open water configuration to streamline the stage bottles.

The Armadillo CCR kit was developed and designed for a single purpose: to eliminate dangling bailout bottles. The Armadillo CCR kit can be used with any rebreather to position the bailout bottles along the diver's body out of the way, in the slipstream of their shoulders.

Q: Tell us how you handle your bailout tanks.

The Armadillo Exploration side mount harness is used as a base harness/wing for many rebreathers (from RB-80, to Kiss, Megalodon, Hammerhead, Inspiration/Evolution, rEvo). One of the unique characteristics of the Armadillo setup is that the rebreather can be "clipped/unclipped" from the harness underwater leaving the diver with a fully functional side mount rig for further penetration/exploration.

The Armadillo Exploration side mount harness is made in a single size. It fits most divers, since all webbing is adjustable, but very small or petite divers will find it uncomfortable due to its length. The Armadillo CCR kit has no weak points. It is perfect! But seriously, the Hammerhead CCR side mount configuration is rather expensive due to the cost of the O_2 cage and round O_2 bottle with a special DIN valve.

Q: What are the weakest points of your system?

Q: What modifications or changes are you considering for the future of your current system and why?

We're building an Armadillo Exploration side mount harness with replaceable wings and a butt

plate to fit any size diver. The incorporated climbing harness is a new feature. Armadillo CCR kit - No changes at all! It is perfect! The Hammerhead CCR side mount configuration will have a smaller Bailout Valve (BOV) and a selection of Back Mounted Counterlungs (BMCLs) as well as a better, less expensive cage and O_2 bottle.

More and more divers will adopt side mount diving as it will allow them to go further and with less effort. The category of side mount CCRs will grow substantially when people discover how streamlined and effortless diving with a side mount CCR can be.

Wes Skiles

Owner, Karst Productions Inc.

DIVE RITE NOMAD OPEN CIRCUIT

HD Cinematographer Wes Skiles was a pioneer in the development of side mount equipment for cave exploration. His gear continued to evolve over time as his diving took him on new and interesting paths. For over a decade, he used the Dive Rite TransPac and Nomad side mount for his base. A dedicated "tinkerer," Skiles continued to assist in the development of new features with Lamar Hires. His rig is represented here in photographs taken a month before his untimely passing, in July 2010.

Jill Heinerth

Owner, Heinerth Productions Inc.

NOMAD SIDEMOUNT AND MODIFIED CCR

My first side mount rig was a pink Sherwood BCD equipped with bicycle inner tubes! It was quite a sight. When the TransPac first came out, I was eager to switch. Still using inner tubes as bungees, this was a far more comfortable and better trimmed rig. As it has evolved, the fit has improved and the wing shape has been modified to provide more balanced trim. Finally, the larger capacity lift was a must for me when working with large, negative cinema lights. When I dive with 95 cft tanks and carry two heavy cinema lights for long filming dives, I need the high lift capacity to stay afloat.

For me, diving side mount is a tool. I have applied that technology to my CCR diving to trim up my tanks. My pet peeve in CCR diving is seeing people whose tanks drag across the reef or cave floor almost perpendicular to their body. Side mount configuration solves this problem instantly. I wish more folks would incorporate these lessons into all their diving.

Q: Please offer a brief history on the evolution of your kit.

Butterfly D-ring instead of butt plate for CCR.

Q: What modifications have you made to your system as it was delivered?

I have made very few modifications to the original Nomad unit. I'm not a fan of the tank choker system, but rather, prefer to literally hang my tank valves in the bungees. Once the valves are properly oriented, they can be doffed and donned very easily. On my rebreather side mount systems, I have eliminated the Nomad butt plate and replaced it with a simple butterfly D-ring. This seems to be more durable and actually gets the tanks tucked in a little better at their base.

When I dive my side mount rig in open water, I face the SPGs straight up. If the tanks are 95 cft or larger, I tuck those SPGs under a small piece of bicycle inner tube that is on the shoulder. That pulls them in close. On my rebreather, I wear the SPGs down, since I don't need to keep a close eye on pressure in bailout tanks. For that reason, I love swivel first stages. I don't have to reconfigure, just spin them around for one or the other type of diving.

Q: What is the strongest point of your unit?

I think the fit of the Nomad is its strongest point. I can comfortably dive or walk through the jungle with tanks on. For women, and their short torsos, it seems to allow for the best customized fit. Not everyone realizes that every single component of a TransPac can be sized to make for ideal fit. I also like using cam bands instead of stainless hardware. I can travel without needing tools and easily switch to single tank use if needed.

Q: What is the weakest point of your unit?

I seem to be wearing out the fabric connections to the tiny D-Rings on the back of the rig, where the bungees connect. Mind you, this has taken a decade of grinding. That said, the bungees occasionally separate from their clips over time and that is an annoying failure when suiting up. As a result, I plan on switching back to either a bicycle inner tube bungee or a fabric-sewn loop that has fewer failure points.

Again, my biggest beef in CCR and OC diving is people who carry their stage or bailout bottles traditionally clipped to D-rings that leave the tanks almost perpendicular to the body. They might be able to get away with this form in open water, but it damages caves and wrecks unnecessarily. I hope that more people learn from side mount divers how to better trim their bailout and stage tanks and closely review the horizontal profile in the water.

I think side mount diving has taken off because of its comfort and versatility. I believe we will see the virtual end to diving back mounted doubles. It simply isn't practical. When a diver switches from open water single tank diving to side mounted doubles, it is more cost effective and feels completely natural. They seem to pick up excellent buoyancy and trim faster than people who dive back mounts.

Q: Where do you see side mount diving technology going in regard to future equipment?

Side exhaust regs won't purge in high flow, are low profile in restrictions and stow neatly under inner tubes.

I always have a spare tank leash in my pocket in case a bungee breaks or to use as a tether.

129

Steve Bogaerts

Owner, GoSideMount.com
DEVELOPER OF THE RAZOR HARNESS

Q: Why did you develop this system?

The Razor Harness is for use on side-mount / no-mount exploration dives in very restricted caves, where every piece of extra equipment can become a hindrance or hazard.

The system evolved over time as the exploration dives became more challenging and demanded more from both diver and equipment. The current system is the distillation of years of trial and error. That experience refined and streamlined equipment, skill sets and procedures.

Q: How is this different than other rigs?

The Razor Harness is at the heart of this system and is the foundation of all the "Bogarthian" side mount procedures. To get the full benefit from your Razor Harness you need to understand and implement the entire Bogarthian Side Mount Philosophy. This philosophy is holistic in approach and is designed from the inside out so that as additional layers of equipment are added there is no change in the core equipment, equipment placement, procedures or skill sets.

Q: What are the pros of your system?

The Razor Harness is simple and elegant, with 2 continuous pieces of webbing and 1 closure point. It is simple, strong, rugged, reliable, low profile and extremely minimalist in design. It fits like a glove and is very comfortable to wear.

The Razor will fit anyone no matter what their physical size or shape and is quick and easy to set up and adjust so that each individual diver gets a custom fit using standardized hardware.

The Razor can be adjusted at several points to ensure the optimal fit for each individual.

Each of the shoulder straps / waist straps can be adjusted at the Mini Back Plate. The length of the Lumbar / Crotch Strap can be adjusted at the Delta Shoulder Plate. The height of the Waist / Hip strap can be adjusted at the Mini Back Plate. All the attachment points such as D-rings on the Razor Harness can be adjusted quickly and easily to allow personalized positioning of equipment placement. Extra attachment points can be added easily if required.

Weight can be added to exactly where you need it on the Razor Harness to optimize trim.

The harness can easily be adjusted so that the lower attachment point for the side mount tanks is either at the waist or lower at the hips.

The optimum positioning will depend on a number of factors including individual diver preference, the length of the diver's torso, the length of the side-mount tanks being used and the overall weight distribution and trim of the diver and their total equipment load.

I am currently working on a modular buoyancy control system specifically to go with the Razor Harness. When I first started using the Razor Harness I was diving it without any kind of BCD, controlling my buoyancy with just lung volume. That worked out okay just diving with two aluminum 80 side mount tanks although at the start of the dive, when the tanks were full, I had to dive at the top of my lung volume and it did not really become comfortable until the tank pressures dropped 500 psi and the tanks became a bit lighter. I really needed a small amount of lift to compensate for the weight of the gas in the tanks at the start of the dive but did not want to add a large and bulky BCD.

In one of my "Eureka" moments I decided to try out a hydration bag that I had lying around as a BCD. The 2 liter volume gave me 4.5 lbs of additional lift. I wrapped the Camelbak horizontally around my lower back over my Razor Harness and held it in place by attaching a bungee cord to one side, running that around my waist and through the front loop of my crotch strap and clipping it off to the other side of the Camelbak with a small snap bolt. I inflated it orally through the bite-on mouthpiece of the drinking tube and dumped air out of it by pinching the mouthpiece between my thumb and forefinger while holding the drinking tube up.

I called it the "BAT Wing" which stands for Buoyancy And Trim Wing.

The most important reason for me to have my BAT Wing over my harness is the ability to easily and quickly remove/replace it underwater while diving if necessary. When I got to no-mount areas I could either take it off altogether and leave it behind or wrap it around my butt mounted tank to get it neutral and make towing the tank easier.

While this system is very, very good I have a few ideas that I hope will improve it further.

At the moment I am in the process of developing a commercially viable modular BC system along the same principles specifically for the Razor Harness and hope to have something available very soon.

Lamar Hires

Owner, Lamartek Inc., dba Dive Rite

NOMAD SIDE MOUNT AND OPTIMA CCR

Dive Rite offers two Nomad side mount systems. Both are based on the TransPac harness and the wings are adaptations from previous side mount systems that we produced as well as back mount systems. The Nomad EXP is a one-piece harness/wing/butt plate system designed for convenience and value. It is for cave or open water side mount. The Nomad XT consists of separate harness/wing/butt plate components and incorporates SuperFabric technology to create a rugged, tear-resistant outer shell. The Nomad XT is our "off-road" version of the Nomad that stands up to the wear and tear of the serious side mount explorer.

Q: Describe the base of your system.

Historically, side mounting was for extreme technical divers who used this configuration to penetrate small sections of cave. It actually began in England with dry cavers who had to traverse partially submerged sections of cave, called sumps. Side mount was simply an easier method for carrying tanks from one sump to the next. In the 1980s, a group of us in north Florida started using side mount to explore small cave passages. Wes Skiles, Mark Long, Ron Simmons, Woody Jasper, and I were pushing tiny tentacles of large cave systems thought to be tapped out, along with a myriad of small caves that had never been attempted.

The Nomad evolved over the years based on my explorations in Florida as well as observing the modifications that my dive buddies made to their rigs. The genesis of the Nomad itself came from an

Q: Please give a brief history on the evolution of this configuration.

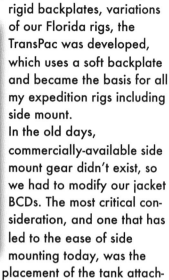

expedition in the remote regions of Japan in 1996. After two failed attempts to push the cave using rigid backplates, variations of our Florida rigs, the TransPac was developed, which uses a soft backplate and became the basis for all my expedition rigs including side mount.

In the old days, commercially-available side mount gear didn't exist, so we had to modify our jacket BCDs. The most critical consideration, and one that has led to the ease of side mounting today, was the placement of the tank attachment point. What we learned over time is that moving the tank attachment point lower on the diver's body gave us more control of the tank and kept the tank under the arm rather than out-in-front riding like a stage bottle. The waist on a Jacket BCD tends to be several inches above the bottom of the jacket, so we couldn't place a D-ring on the waist belt and get a low connection; we had to find alternate solutions. Gary Walton came up with the idea for an extension on the waist belt, called an "egg beater" – a 2-inch D-ring welded to a 6-inch rod that was welded to a steel belt slide for his wife Kay. The welded assembly resembled the beater of an electric mixer and when attached to the waist belt, it lowered the mounting point of the bottle a good several inches.

Brett Hemphill came up with the idea for today's butt plate with rails that allow the tanks to "float" next to the diver instead of being held tight when clipped into D-rings at the waist. Side mount divers need this mobility when squeezing into a tight spot as they look for just a bit more wiggle room. If tanks are held fast to the side of the diver, mobility becomes limited and in some cases can risk a diver getting jammed as the tanks "A-frame" away from the diver's body and prevent the diver from backing out of a one-way restriction. Brett gave us permission to incorporate the butt plate into the Nomad.

In the early years, we preferred light weight cylinders, such as steel 72s. With the shift to heavy steel tanks, jacket-style rigs and smaller volume wings can't handle the load of large tanks, especially when staging, and this began to limit side mount exploration. Dive Rite designed a wing to give side mounters the lift they need to carry the heavy bottles. Both the Nomad EXP and Nomad XT have 60 lbs of lift for steel 95s and 108s, plus stages. We also added a flexible bungee system. In the early days, my friend Woody Jasper came up with one continuous piece of bicycle inner tube that ran across the back from one bottle to the next. It worked because it was all we had, but the downside is if you damage the bungee you lose both tanks; there's no safety in it. The Nomad uses two separate bungees for added security. They can be attached a lot of different ways to the tanks, giving the side mount diver added flexibility.

Since launching in 2007, the Nomad has been modified in only three ways. First, we made the sizing broader to fit both tall individuals who are 6'5"

Q: What significant modifications to the base harness/wing have you made?

and taller and short individuals who are 5'4" or less. Second, we added additional lift from 50 lbs to 60 lbs to accommodate the explorer who wears heavy steel tanks, plus multiple stage bottles, however our Gusset Control System allows the diver to limit lift when diving smaller tanks such as aluminum 80s. Third, we now have a ring bungee system that makes sizing the bungees much easier, plus you can don your tanks very quickly, even while treading water off the side of a boat. The ring bungee system integrates safety clips so divers won't stress the bungee if they need to enter/exit the water with tanks attached.

Q: What do you feel is the strongest point of your kit in regard to side mount diving in small caves?

Two points. First, and foremost, the Nomad has more than two decades of evolution diving in side mount caves. The name "Nomad" is the name of our current side mount system, but it is not a new system. Prior to launching the Nomad, Dive Rite had the BC Junior, Sport Wing and Trek side mount systems. As explorations demanded more from the gear, the Nomad was born. What this means to the end user is that the Nomad's design is a well thought-out combination of decades of learning from designs that didn't quite work. For example, the ring bungee/choker system is designed so that the bottles float and have some movement alongside the diver. This consideration is critical...not all restrictions permit a stiff bottle configuration. In fact, most restrictions are irregular so the bottles must be able to shift and find that "sweet spot" to let the diver pass through. Some rigs today are repeating our mistakes of the past by having rigid bottle placement that causes the bottles to flare at the bottom. This presents problems for the diver, especially when backing out of a restriction.

Second, the Nomad is designed for side mount diving in a diverse array of environments. It can handle a variety of

cylinder sizes and quickly convert to back mount or single tank if necessary during an exploration. Some of the rigs you see on the market today are designed for a specific environment or tailored to the needs of the designer. These rigs are limited by their lift or their versatility since they were created to meet the needs of the designer, not the broader dive market. Not so with the Nomad. It is the culmination of years of experience and is a truly versatile rig.

Because the Nomad incorporates the TransPac, it is completely adaptable for back mount diving. A diver does not need to make any alternations to the Nomad. Simply attach the rig to their double tanks using the 11-inch on center bolt spacing. The Nomad even has two sets of grommets for trim. We've seen a huge trend in back mount divers side mounting stage bottles with the butt plate/bungee system and it works well to streamline the diver and improve efficiency in the water.

Q: What do you feel is the strongest point of your kit in regard to side mount diving in back mount sized caves?

Both the Nomad EXP and Nomad XT have 60 lbs of lift to work with all but the very heaviest of back mount cylinders. The Nomad XT is modular, so the butt plate can be removed or a different wing can be used for back mount if desired. This is important for divers who travel and don't want to carry separate rigs. The Nomad can be worn for just about any dive or simply make a few adjustments to reconfigure the base harness system. Because it is designed originally for exploration, the Nomad can easily adjust from side mount to doubles or singles – an explorer doesn't always know what type of dive lies ahead and the principles behind a flexible rig mean the non-explorer also benefits from this flexibility.

When side mounting in open water the key is to be able to secure and remove bottles while floating at the surface. You can do this with the Nomad by using the bungee ring system. Remember, bungees

Q: What do you feel is the strongest point of your kit for diving in open water?

137

are meant to ride the tanks under the arm, not to support the weight of the tank at the surface. The safety ring preserves the integrity of the bungee and instead places the weight on the choker/clip when attached to the harness D-ring. There is no fumbling to try to stretch bungee around the tank neck to attach the bottle, nor does the diver have to worry about the bungee slipping off mid-dive. The Nomad Weight Plate can be added if additional weight is needed by the diver.

The Nomad also allows for single, back mounted cylinder diving by using two cam straps woven through the 2-inch webbing on the TransPac harness. Weight pockets can be inverted on the belt and lift controlled using the Gusset Control System on the face of the wing. During cave expeditions in Japan, we wore two small cylinders (5.25-inch diameter) side by side using cam straps. This gave us the redundancy we needed, yet a lightweight rig for quick reconnaissance missions or the ability to easily side mount the tight stuff.

The unit can be converted for single tank use.

Q: How does the unit convert for CCR bailout?

138

Side mount is ideal for CCR since it allows the diver to carry bailout bottles next to him instead of in front. One of the challenges for most CCR divers is that there is so much gear in front of the diver such as the loop, counterlungs, etc. Having bailout bottles hung in a traditional stage rigging, clipped to a harness and waist D-rings means more gear out in front. The Nomad is especially helpful in this regard because of its ring bungee/choker system. The CCR diver simply clips into the butt plate rail and then the bungee and is ready to go. No fumbling to stretch the bungee around the bottle and get to that hard-to-reach shoulder D-ring.

Most CCR divers combat the natural heads-up buoyancy of the rebreather. The Nomad is designed to give lift preferentially at the hips helping to trim the CCR diver. Lift can be modified using the Gusset Control System, if needed. If more real estate is needed on the waist, the CCR diver can release the waist belt loops of the Nomad wing so that it flares freely, instead of staying tucked as is necessary when side mounting.

Brian Kakuk

Owner, Bahamas Underground

ARMADILLO SIDE MOUNT

Q: What is the base of your system?

I've been using the Armadillo since the first production run. Currently I have an A-2 model that I have modified a bit. I do use various versions of the DiveRite Nomad(s) for specific types of dives, but my everyday use is the Armadillo A-2 for teaching, guiding and most exploration.

Q: What significant modifications to the base harness/wing have you made and why?

I added D-rings to the back of the harness/BCD system and I have sewn in a section of ½ inch tubular webbing to better route the dump cord for the upper dump valve. I also added an old style Dive Rite Trek Side Mount Bungee System that was sewn out of 2" tubular webbing, 1" flat elastic bands (similar to elastic dive computer wrist bands now), and a section of 2-inch nylon webbing with stainless belt slides on each end. The nylon webbing is laced through one of the slots in the upper back of the Armadillo on the outside, and then the 2-inch tubular webbing with the flat elastic loops on the ends are laced into the belt slides and adjusted to appropriate fit for the individual diver. I hope that Dive Rite will begin manufacturing these bungee systems again as I feel they are superior to what is being used today and most importantly, being flat, and on the outside of the wing, they help keep down the shoulder bubble that is a snag point on almost all side mount BCDs manufactured today.

I added a clip system to the power inflator that allows me to clip the inflator hose across my chest, placing it in the center of my chest above my sternum. This makes the power inflator "no-handed" and accessible from either hand.

I added a right angle D-ring designed for re-breather harnesses to give access to D-rings that have been covered by chest mounted counterlungs. This D-ring gives me great separation of second stage regulators when multiple second stages (more than two) are used in stage diving.

Again, the shoulder bubble profile has been greatly reduced with the use of a flat, external bun-gee system. The Armadillo has incredibly rugged construction. Small profile is both a strong point and weak point of this system. Smaller profile means much more snag resistance, but also means less lift

Q: What do you feel is the strongest point of your kit in regard to side mount diving in side mount caves?

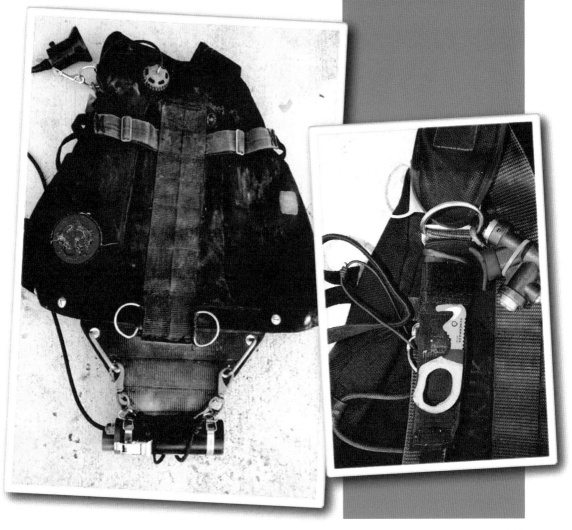

141

than some of the other systems. My equipment choices are mission specific. If I want to go into small cave, I use the Armadillo.

I feel that the Armadillo, rigged in this fashion, has the smallest profile of all of the off-the-rack side mount systems.

Q: What about back mount caves?

The system is at home in large or small caves. The harness can be attached to back mount CCRs with side mounted bail out.

Q: And open water?

This system works well for side mounting in open water, for reef, wall and wreck diving with side mounted cylinders as well as being adaptable to single cylinder use simply by inserting two cam bands through the available slots on the back.

Q: Tell us about CCR bailout adaptability.

The new CCR side mount kit works well on my Megalodon CCR for streamlining bailout cylinders.

Q: What is the weakest point of your system?

Lift and available sizing. Sizing has been addressed by Golem Gear and options will be available soon.

None at present, but I'm always learning from others, including my students, as well as coming up with my own ideas. It doesn't matter if you are one of the "Mole Tribe" or a new cave diver, show me what works, show me what is safe, and show me how I can go smaller, longer and deeper, and I'll do what ever it takes with regard to harness and other kit modifications.

LIGHTS

In the past, one of the biggest hurdles in regard to profile was primary light battery packs. This has changed drastically with current HID and LED models, and continues to get even better. I look forward to a handheld LED that out performs current 10-watt HID in both brightness and focus. Current LED 800 lumen handhelds are great touring lights with broad soft beams, but explorers need a small, focused beam to penetrate down possible leads in the cave.

SIDE MOUNT CCR

In my opinion, the entire future of underwater cave exploration is going to make leaps and bounds with the design of safe, efficient side mounted CCR units. My goal is to get rid of all OC bailout and use only two side mounted CCR units breathed to thirds. The exploration potential for such a kit is limitless in terms of time, cave passage size and depth.

Q: What modifications are you considering?

Q: Where do you see side mount diving technology going in regard to future equipment systems?

CONCLUSIONS

CHAPTER 12

In Conclusion

Side mount configuration is rapidly transforming the way many technical divers approach their craft. Not just for explorers any more, side mount diving is a safe and logical alternative to back mounted doubles in diving environments from caves to open water to wrecks Yet, unlike some other aspects of technical or cave diving, there is no perfect solution to gear configuration and technique. There are simply too many mission specific uses that require variations of the base configuration. The average sump diver needs an extremely streamlined harness combined with small cylinders and perhaps little need for additional buoyancy. But lacking a contingency for buoyancy, the same harness system would be considered unsafe for open water diving. Furthermore, the variety of body morphologies demands a unique center of balance and fit for every individual.

Be it from the mouths of doctors or mechanics, we have heard the same mantra for years, "use the proper tool for the job." Today's side mount diver has many different tools to choose from, each offering unique strengths and weaknesses. There are some tools that suffice for several environments, but other harnesses that specialize in one type of diving. It is up to the individual diver to decide which tool is the most suitable.

The experts presented in this text are trailblazers in the discipline of cave diving. The constant evolution of their systems based on their own ideas, as well as those of their peers and students, has led to a move-

Lamar Hires and Tom Morris prepare for a dive.

ment within the diving industry to embrace side mount diving in all its forms as a safe and comfortable tool for exploring our underwater world. Bringing a focus on detail and conservatism, their lessons cross over to other disciplines in diving.

The typical open water recreational diver has no need for another cylinder in order to drift around a 30-foot deep tropical reef. But, once the open water diver decides to carry an extra cylinder, they are now delving into the realm of technical diving. Increased exposure to cold, nitrogen, oxygen, depths and distances from their starting point create the need for formal dive plans and additional training. And most would argue that the additional planning offers plenty of reward. Stability, an independent/redundant gas supply and a streamlined profile give the side mount diver a viable option for accessing areas of their chosen underwater environment not previously obtainable with conventional back mounted equipment.

Instructor Rich Courtney and John Fodor drop through Devil's Eye on their Friday night dive.

We cannot overemphasize that this text should not be considered as stand-alone training. There is no replacement for formal instruction by an experienced, qualified and certified side mount instructor who makes a point of keeping up with current techniques and technology. Their dives outside of teaching will have built a foundation of lessons that reveal the intricacies and hazards of your specialized diving interest.

We hope that your journey into side mount diving, whether in open water, within the engine room of some deep wreck, or grinding through underground labyrinths as a subaqueous spelunker, will be one of safe and comfortable exploration. We also hope that your involvement with this form of diving will lead to smart, experience-based innovations of your own. Please take the time to share your ideas and innovations with the rest of the side mount community. After all, that's how the experts got where they are now.

Safe diving,
Brian and Jill

Rick Palm and Craig Walters dive together as a mixed team, regularly rehearsing their emergency procedures.

—

Printed in Great Britain
by Amazon.co.uk, Ltd.,
Marston Gate.